Elizabeth Connor, MLS, AHIP
Editor

An Introduction to Reference Services in Academic Libraries

Pre-publication
REVIEWS,
COMMENTARIES,
EVALUATIONS . . .

"This book is a refreshing treatise on reference services in academic libraries. Editor Elizabeth Connor has taken a new approach to the basic principles as well as the 'hot' issues in reference work by compiling both essays and case studies contributed by professionals in the field. The timely and sometimes humorous case studies address real-life situations and projects of interest to anyone involved in academic library reference. Subjects range from traditional in-person reference services to models for virtual reference, chat reference, and reference triage. The essays are insightful and stimulating, and address issues such as diversity in libraries, the history of reference librarianship, serving unusual patrons, promotion and tenure, and the emerging 'new librarian.'

Unique to the work are the supplementary exercises suggested at the end of each case study or essay. Designed to engage readers and promote critical thinking, the short assignments invite readers to put what they have learned to practical use by applying new ideas to their own work environments. This work, rich in innovative material, is an excellent resource for graduate students, librarians at any career stage, newcomers to academic librarianship, library support staff, and others interested in understanding reference services in the academic environment."

Laura Townsend Kane, MLIS, AHIP
Assistant Director for Information Services,
School of Medicine Library,
University of South Carolina

More pre-publication
REVIEWS, COMMENTARIES, EVALUATIONS . . .

"This book is filled with well-written, insightful, and thought-provoking essays that are essential reading for both aspiring and seasoned academic reference librarians. Practical and sometimes humorous case studies and essays highlight almost every type of academic reference service in a variety of library sizes. Of particular importance are the studies that assess and explore the impact technology is having on reference service and how the reference librarian's role is changing as a result. The book's broad range both illustrates and reflects the multidimensional role of academic reference librarians and the wide variety of academic environments in which they work. New librarians will see the challenges and rewards of academic reference service, and seasoned librarians will gain valuable insight into the professional lives and experiences of their peers. Librarians have much to gain from these diverse and authentic voices from the field."

Helene E. Gold, MLS, MEd
Electronic Services Librarian,
Associate Professor, Eckerd College,
St. Petersburg, Florida

"Practical, relevant, and cheeky, this book covers issues, challenges, and work of reference in a variety of academic settings. Using case studies and provocative essays with exercises following each chapter, this text provides excellent examples to use in library and information science education and training. I recommend this be used in graduate programs of LIS to teach reference functions in an academic library beyond information sources used. The case studies are real-life based, diverse in types of institutions, and the issues are current and relevant. Just as in real life, cases represent successes, failures, disappointments, and the bemusing in academic reference librarianship. I also recommend this book as an on-the-job training manual for skills to be refreshed or newly learned."

Lorna Peterson, PhD
Associate Professor,
University of Buffalo

"This book is the first in a series of Haworth Press publications that will serve as introductory textbooks to library services in academic libraries. However, it is not a textbook in the traditional sense. This book presents the readers with a series of situations that beginning librarians are likely to encounter in their first position. Drawing on actual and fictional scenarios, it presents the reader with thought-provoking questions about instruction and reference service. Topics covered include reference desk design, marketing reference services, virtual reference, and cost-effectiveness of reference service. The second part of the book presents a series of essays about topics such as diversity, respect, and the future of librarianship. Each chapter is followed by a series of questions that the reader can use to help interpret and understand the issues."

David A. Tyckoson
Head of Public Services,
Henry Madden Library,
California State University–Fresno

More pre-publication
REVIEWS, COMMENTARIES, EVALUATIONS . . .

"**W**e should all be so lucky to have such engaging texts to use with our students. This book takes the often uninspiring combination of case studies and topical essays and breathes new life into it via topicality and humor. There is a solid mix of short and long, data-packed and more anecdotal, and techie and not-so techie, clearly showing a careful selection process."

Jessamyn West, MLib
Adult Ed Technology Coordinator,
Randolph Technical Career Center

"**C**onsisting of a broad and interesting cross-section of essays and case studies, this book describes the range of issues confronting librarians responsible for planning reference services in academic libraries. The case studies and essays reveal that a spectrum of concepts as diverse as heuristics, space planning, leadership princi-ples, human behavior, the tenets of good educational practice, and the use of appropriate technology are applicable to crafting excellent reference services and practice. The book is a testimony to the determination of practitioners in the field to face the challenge of developing reference services that are practice, ingenious, appropriate, and client-based. The content is useful for both the novice and the expert, and no doubt would be used differently according to need. Newcomers to the field will discover the myriad of issues facing professionals who plan reference services. Many practicing librarians will encounter some familiar experiences and are as likely to have their choice of solution confirmed as to gain insight into new ways of thinking."

Ernesta E. Greenidge, MLS, AHIP
Head, Medical Sciences Library,
The University of the West Indies
at St. Augustine, Trinidad and Tobago

The Haworth Information Press®
An Imprint of The Haworth Press
New York • London • Oxford

An Introduction
to Reference Services
in Academic Libraries

The Haworth Information Press®
*Haworth Series in Introductory Information
Science Textbooks*

An Introduction to Reference Services in Academic Libraries edited
by Elizabeth Connor

Titles of Related Interest

*A Guide to Developing End User Education Programs in Medical
Libraries* by Elizabeth Connor

Libraries and Google^{SM} edited by William Miller and Rita M. Pellen

Licensing in Libraries: Practical and Ethical Aspects edited by Karen
Rupp-Serrano

Managing Digital Resources in Libraries edited by Audrey Fenner

Reference Librarianship: Notes from the Trenches by Charles Anderson
and Peter Sprenkle

Computers in Libraries: An Introduction for Library Technicians by Katie
Wilson

An Introduction
to Reference Services
in Academic Libraries

Elizabeth Connor, MLS, AHIP
Editor

The Haworth Information Press®
An Imprint of The Haworth Press
New York • London • Oxford

For more information on this book or to order, visit
http://www.haworthpress.com/store/product.asp?sku=5634

or call 1-800-HAWORTH (800-429-6784) in the United States and Canada
or (607) 722-5857 outside the United States and Canada

or contact orders@HaworthPress.com

Published by

The Haworth Information Press®, an imprint of The Haworth Press, Inc., 10 Alice Street, Binghamton, NY 13904-1580.

PUBLISHER'S NOTE
The development, preparation, and publication of this work has been undertaken with great care. However, the Publisher, employees, editors, and agents of The Haworth Press are not responsible for any errors contained herein or for consequences that may ensue from use of materials or information contained in this work. The Haworth Press is committed to the dissemination of ideas and information according to the highest standards of intellectual freedom and the free exchange of ideas. Statements made and opinions expressed in this publication do not necessarily reflect the views of the Publisher, Directors, management, or staff of The Haworth Press, Inc., or an endorsement by them.

Cover design by Jennifer M. Gaska.
TR: 9.21.06

Library of Congress Cataloging-in-Publication Data

Connor, Elizabeth, MLS.
    An introduction to reference services in academic libraries / Elizabeth Connor.
        p. cm.
    Includes bibliographic references and index.
    ISBN-13: 978-0-7890-2957-7 (hard : alk. paper)
    ISBN-10: 0-7890-2957-X (hard : alk. paper)
    ISBN-13: 978-0-7890-2958-4 (soft : alk. paper)
    ISBN-10: 0-7890-2958-8 (soft : alk. paper)
1. Academic libraries—Reference services. 2. Academic libraries—Reference services—United States—Case studies. 3. Reference services (Libraries)—Problems, exercises, etc. I. Connor, Elizabeth, MLS.

Z675.U5I598 2006
025.52777—dc22

                                                                                        2006008061

To Alix G. Darden, who epitomizes active learning
and the scholarship of teaching and learning

CONTENTS

ABOUT THE EDITOR

Elizabeth Connor, MLS, AHIP, is Assistant Professor of Library Science and Science Liaison, The Citadel, Charleston, South Carolina, and is a distinguished member of the Academy of Health Information Professionals. She has extensive experience planning, designing, managing, and serving as consultant for library renovation and building projects at several institutions, and has a keen interest in ergonomics and collaborative workplaces. She is author of several peer-reviewed articles about medical informatics, electronic resources, search engines, and chat reference, and has written more than sixty book reviews for *Library Journal, Against the Grain, Bulletin of the Medical Library Association, Journal of the Medical Library Association, Medical Reference Services Quarterly,* and *The Post and Courier.* Ms. Connor has edited the *Internet Guide to Travel Health,* the *Internet Guide to Food Safety and Security, A Guide to Developing End User Education Programs in Medical Libraries,* and *Planning, Renovating, Expanding, and Constructing Library Facilities in Hospitals, Academic Medical Centers, and Health Organizations,* all published by The Haworth Press, Inc.

An Introduction to Reference Services in Academic Libraries
© 2006 by The Haworth Press, Inc. All rights reserved.
doi:10.1300/5634_a

Contributors

Michael J. Bell, PhD (mbell@elmhurst.edu) is Vice President of Academic Affairs and Dean of Faculty at Elmhurst College in Elmhurst, Illinois.

Paul Blobaum, MA, MS (p-blobaum@govst.edu) is University Professor and Reference Librarian at Governors State University Library in University Park, Illinois.

Christopher Nelson Cox, MLS, MA (coxcn@uwec.edu) is Assistant Director of McIntyre Library at the University of Wisconsin in Eau Claire.

Valeda Frances Dent, MSW, MILS (vdent@hunter.cuny.edu) is Assistant Professor and Head, Reference Department at Hunter College City University of New York in New York City.

Rusty Gaspard, BA, MLIS (rgaspard@lsua.edu) is Assistant Librarian at the James C. Bolton Library of Louisiana State University in Alexandria, Louisiana.

Tammy S. Guerrero, MLS (guerrero@calumet.purdue.edu) is Circulation/Reference Librarian at Purdue University Calumet in Hammond, Indiana.

John E. Holberg, MA, MSt (holberg@covenant.edu) is Instructional Services and Reference Librarian at Covenant College in Lookout Mountain, Georgia.

Ned Kraft (kraftno@state.gov) is Acquisitions Team Leader of the Ralph J. Bunche Library at the U. S. Department of State in Washington, DC. In this book, Dr. Kraft uses the pseudonyms Mary Mee, Marilyn Schoot-Castle, and Miron Stenche.

James Langan, MLS (jlangan@pitt.edu) is Reference Librarian at Owen Library of the University of Pittsburgh at Johnstown in Johnstown, Pennsylvania.

An Introduction to Reference Services in Academic Libraries
© 2006 by The Haworth Press, Inc. All rights reserved.
doi:10.1300/5634_b

Matthew R. Marsteller, MSLS (matthewm@andrew.cmu.edu) is Physics and Math Librarian at Carnegie Mellon University in Pittsburgh, Pennsylvania.

Mark L. McCallon, EdD, MLS (mccallonm@acu.edu) is Assistant Director of the Margaret and Herman Brown Library at Abilene Christian University in Abilene, Texas.

Mary Mee is Reference Librarian at Fraught Memorial Library of Darkmound University, which is located somewhere in northeast New York State. Mee is a pseudonym for Ned Kraft.

Jolene M. Miller, MLS, AHIP (jomiller@meduohio.edu) is Reference/Education Librarian at the Mulford Library of the Medical University of Ohio in Toledo, Ohio.

Marlene A. Porter, MLn (mporter2@meduohio.edu) is Head of Information Services at the Mulford Library of the Medical University of Ohio in Toledo, Ohio.

Debra Cox Rollins, BA, MLIS (drollins@lsua.edu) is Assistant Librarian at the James C. Bolton Library of Louisiana State University in Alexandria, Louisiana.

Linda Loos Scarth, EdD (lscarth@mmc.mtmercy.edu) is Reference Librarian at Mount Mercy College in Cedar Rapids, Iowa.

Marilyn Schoot-Castle is Reference Librarian at Fraught Memorial Library of Darkmound University, which is located somewhere in northeast New York State. Schoot-Castle is a pseudonym for Ned Kraft.

Paula M. Smith, MSIS (pms20@psu.edu) is Assistant Librarian at Pennsylvania State University Abington Campus in Abington, Pennsylvania.

Miron Stenche is an MLS candidate who works at Fraught Memorial Library of Darkmound University, which is located somewhere in northeast New York State. Stenche is a pseudonym for Ned Kraft.

Susan Swords Steffen, MALS (susanss@elmhurst.edu) is Director of A. C. Buehler Library at Elmhurst College in Elmhurst, Illinois.

Susan Ware, MSLS (saw4@psu.edu) is Reference and Instruction Librarian at Pennsylvania State University, Delaware County in Media, Pennsylvania.

Preface

This is the first in a series of introductory textbooks intended to serve as an instructional framework for teaching and learning the principles of reference services in academic libraries. This book's real-life, hypothetical, and sometimes humorous examples can be used to guide discussions, plan assignments, and engage learners in the classroom or workplace.

Written for graduate students, entry-level librarians, newcomers to academic librarianship, library support staff, and others interested in academic reference services, this book relates specific examples of library work within the greater context of library practice, and encourages readers to think, reflect, prepare to write, and discuss.

In September and October 2004, the editor issued a call for participation on several discussion lists that invited academic reference librarians to submit abstracts for a forthcoming textbook. Contributors were selected based on the quality of their submissions with the idea that the editor would weave together the different case studies and essays with active learning activities. Completed case studies and essays were submitted and revised by March 2005.

Experienced academic librarian contributors have provided the foundational knowledge needed to understand how reference services are developed, managed, and assessed. Each case study or essay is supplemented by short assignments written by the editor. These assignments require students to think, apply knowledge, work individually or in groups, and analyze issues that face practicing librarians. This approach is based on the seminal work conducted by McWorter which relates Bloom's taxonomy to class content through the use of increasingly complex questions.[1] These activities are intended to help readers construct new knowledge, make meaningful connections with previous knowledge through the use of real-life or imaginary examples, and allow for deeper understanding by requiring the use of higher-order thinking skills. Exercises extend beyond knowl-

An Introduction to Reference Services in Academic Libraries
© 2006 by The Haworth Press, Inc. All rights reserved.
doi:10.1300/5634_c

edge and comprehension of concepts, and focus on analysis, synthesis, and evaluation.[2] Short writing assignments, in particular, engage learners and promote critical thinking. Bean describes writing as a process that communicates "the results of critical thinking."[3]

For example, when reading about virtual reference, it is useful to read other case studies or essays that discuss similar concepts, and complete the suggested exercises following each. Learning activities based on Bloom's taxonomy (knowledge, comprehension, application, analysis, synthesis, and evaluation) were developed for four major subjects (virtual reference, promotion and tenure, reference triage, and relational reference) and are featured in Tables P.1 through P.4.

Active learning activities are effective methods to engage and sustain learning among graduate library science students and practicing librarians. Such activities can help develop evidence-based librarianship skills needed to solve problems and the habits of mind necessary to think like librarians and academic faculty. Readers are encouraged

TABLE P.1. Learning Activities for Virtual Reference—Reading Case Studies 5, 8, and 10

Thinking Levels	Learning Activity
Knowledge	Define virtual reference services.
Comprehension	Explain how virtual reference services complement other library services.
Application	Think of examples of the types of library users served by virtual library services or the types of libraries that offer such services. Are there any patron or library types that are not suited for this approach?
Analysis	Describe the features of the virtual reference services described in the readings.
Synthesis	Develop a set of criteria that can be used to measure the success or failure of virtual reference services.
Evaluation	Using the criteria developed above, compare/contrast the features and relative effectiveness of services described in the readings. Submit the same question to three virtual reference services and compare the interactions and answers.

Adapted from McWhorter, Kathleen T. *Study and Critical Thinking Skills in College,* Fifth Edition. New York: Addison, 2003.

TABLE P.2. Learning Activities for Academic Librarians—Reading Case Studies 6 and 7 and Essays 2, 3, and 7

Thinking levels	Learning activity
Knowledge	Define academic librarian.
Comprehension	List three to five priorities for academic librarians to focus on for promotion and tenure.
Application	Rank the above priorities according to sequence of events (first year, second year, third year, etc.).
Analysis	List two to three specific activities or strategies for each priority ranked above.
Synthesis	Should academic librarians be tenure-track faculty? Why or why not?
Evaluation	Develop a multiyear checklist for newly hired academic librarians to follow that charts and tracks yearly progress related to the priorities, activities, or strategies developed above.

Adapted from McWhorter, Kathleen T. *Study and Critical Thinking Skills in College,* Fifth Edition. New York: Addison, 2003.

TABLE P.3. Learning Activities for Reference Triage—Reading Case Studies 2 and 8 and Essay 5

Thinking levels	Learning activity
Knowledge	Define reference triage.
Comprehension	List three advantages of introducing reference triage in an academic setting.
Application	Draw a diagram or flowchart of how reference triage related to other library services.
Analysis	What types of academic libraries would benefit from this approach? Are there types of academic libraries that would not?
Synthesis	Develop a list of criteria that can be used to compare different ways to handle directional, ready, and in-depth reference questions.
Evaluation	Choose three types of reference services including reference triage. Use the criteria developed above to create a matrix that compares the three types.

Adapted from McWhorter, Kathleen T. *Study and Critical Thinking Skills in College,* Fifth Edition. New York: Addison, 2003.

TABLE P.4. Learning Activities for Relational Reference—Reading Case Studies 2, 4, and 8 and Essay 5

Thinking levels	Learning activity
Knowledge	Define relational reference.
Comprehension	Is relational reference effective? Why or why not?
Application	Think of two or three nonlibrary settings that use a configuration similar to the relational reference model.
Analysis	What types of furniture and equipment could be used to implement relational reference in a small college library? A large research university?
Synthesis	Draw a diagram of an ideal librarian-patron furniture configuration, relative to the entrance, public areas, collections, computers, etc.
Evaluation	Visit three types of libraries, including an academic library, and compare the configuration and location of each library's reference furniture and equipment. Ask the same reference question at each library, and compare the interactions. Were you told, shown, taught, and/or referred?

Adapted from McWhorter, Kathleen T. *Study and Critical Thinking Skills in College,* Fifth Edition. New York: Addison, 2003.

to think about how they can use each chapter's information in the workplace, connect the information to what they already know, and ask questions about what they are reading. The case studies and essays serve as rich material and contexts for understanding reference services in academic libraries and the practices that benefit academic librarians.

NOTES

1. McWhorter, Kathleen T. *Study and Critical Thinking Skills in College,* Fifth Edition. New York: AddisonWesley Longman, Inc., 2003.

2. Bloom, B. S. (Ed.). *Taxonomy of Educational Objectives.* New York: McKay, 1956.

3. Bean, John C. *Engaging Ideas: The Professor's Guide to Integrating Writing, Critical Thinking, and Active Learning in the Classroom.* San Francisco, CA: Jossey-Bass Publishers, 2001, p. 3.

BIBLIOGRAPHY

Anderson, Lorin W. (Ed.). *A Taxonomy for Learning, Teaching, and Assessing: A Revision of Bloom's Taxonomy of Educational Objectives.* New York: Longman, 2001.

Angelo, Thomas A. and Cross, K. Patricia. *Classroom Assessment Techniques: A Handbook for College Teachers,* Second Edition. San Francisco, CA; Jossey-Bass Publishers, 1993.

Association for Library and Information Science Education. *Educating Library and Information Science Professionals for a New Century: The KALIPER Report.* Reston, VA: ALISE, 2000.

Bonwell, Charles C. and Eison, James A. *Active Learning: Creating Excitement in the Classroom.* ASHE-ERIC Higher Education Report 1, 1991.

Brookhart, S. M. *The Art and Science of Classroom Assessment: The Missing Part of Pedagogy.* ASHE-ERIC Higher Education Report 27, 1, 1999.

Choinski, Elizabeth, Mark, Amy E., and Murphey, Missy. Assessment with Rubrics: An Efficient and Objective Means of Assessing Student Outcomes in an Information Resources Class. *Portal: Libraries and the Academy* 3(4) (2003): 563-575.

Cleyle, Susan E. and McGillis, Louise M. *Last One Out Turn Off the Lights: Is This the Future of American and Canadian Libraries?* Lanham, MD: Scarecrow Press, 2005.

Cranton, Patricia *Understanding and Promoting Transformative Learning: A Guide for Educators and Adults.* San Francisco, CA: Jossey-Bass, 1994.

Cranton, Patricia, and Carusetta, Ellen. Reflecting on Teaching: The Influence of Context. *International Journal for Academic Development* 7(2) (2002): 167-176.

Curran, Charles. What Sixty-One Superior LIS Teachers Say About Superior LIS Teaching, Plus Comments from Six Knowledgeable Observers. *Journal of Education for Library and Information Science* 39(3) (1998): 183-194.

Fink, L. Dee. *Creating Significant Learning Experiences: An Integrated Approach to Designing College Courses.* San Francisco, CA: Jossey-Bass, 2003.

Gagne, Robert M. and Driscoll, Marcy Perkins. *Essentials of Learning for Instruction,* Second Edition. Englewood Cliffs, NJ: Prentice Hall, 1988.

Genz, Marcella D. Working the Reference Desk. *Library Trends* 46(3) (1998): 505-525.

Harmin, Merrill. *Inspiring Active Learning: A Handbook for Teachers.* Alexandria, VA: Association for Supervision and Curriculum Development, 1994.

Hutchins, Margaret. *Introduction to Reference Work.* Chicago, IL: American Library Association, 1944.

Katz, William A. *Introduction to Reference Work,* Volume II, Fifth Edition. New York: McGraw-Hill Book Company, 1987.

Killen, Patricia O'Connell. Making Thinking Real Enough to Make It Better: Using Posters to Develop Skills for Constructing Disciplinary Arguments. *Teaching Theology and Religion* 5(4) (2002): 221-226.

McMillan, James H. and Schumacher, Sally. *Research in Education: Evidence-Based Inquiry,* Sixth Edition. Boston, MA: Pearson Education, Inc., 2006.

Metzger, Philip A. An Overview of the History of Library Science Teaching Materials. *Library Trends* 34(1986): 469-488.

Murfin, Marjorie E. and Wynar, Lubomyr R. *Reference Service: An Annotated Bibliographic Guide.* Littleton, CO: Libraries Unlimited, Inc., 1977.

Oblinger, Diana. Boomers, Gen-Xers, and Millennials: Understanding the New Students. *EDUCAUSE Review* July/August (2003): 37-47.

Paul, Richard and Elder, Linda. *Critical Thinking: Tools for Taking Charge of Your Learning and Your Life.* Upper Saddle River, NJ: Prentice Hall, 2001.

Richardson, John V. Jr. Teaching General Reference Work: The Complete Paradigm and Competing Schools of Thought, 1890-1990. *Library Quarterly* 62(1) (1992): 55-89.

Rubin, Richard E. *Foundations of Library and Information Science.* New York: Neal-Schuman Publishers, Inc., 2000.

Wilson, Lizabeth. *Library Use Instruction: Syllabus, Lecture Outlines, Assignments, and Guest Presentations.* Urbana, IL: Graduate School of Library and Information Science, Illinois University, 1985.

PART I:
CASE STUDIES

Case Study 1

Development, Implementation, and Assessment of a Virtual Information Literacy Tutorial on an Urban Campus

Valeda Frances Dent

SETTING

Hunter College, one of a system of nineteen colleges that make up the City University of New York (CUNY), is located in New York City in the borough of Manhattan. CUNY is a major urban university system composed of a combination of two-year colleges, four-year colleges, a law school, and a PhD-granting graduate school. Hunter College is an urban campus, with many students commuting to the college via public transportation. The school has an incredibly diverse student population that mirrors that of the surrounding boroughs, and students hail from a wide variety of racial, cultural, and socioeconomic groups. Approximately 20,000 undergraduate and graduate students in a wide range of liberal arts and professional programs pursue higher education at Hunter College, and more than eighty different countries are represented. Sixty-five percent of Hunter students speak a language other than English at home. Many are the first in their families to attend college, thus students arrive at Hunter with varying research skills and abilities, and divergent levels of information competency. Given these facts, Hunter College librarians thought it important to provide research skills and information for new students at the most basic levels, and the VOILA! (Virtual ORSEM Information Literacy Assessment) project was developed in part to facilitate students' initial interaction with research and the library

An Introduction to Reference Services in Academic Libraries
© 2006 by The Haworth Press, Inc. All rights reserved.
doi:10.1300/5634_01

in a way that was meaningful, nonintimidating, and engaging. This case study highlights the development of VOILA!

The Hunter College Library has been active in providing bibliographic instruction for more than twenty years. Over the course of a three-year period, from 2001 to 2004, librarians taught approximately 900 classes to more than 20,000 students. On average, the instruction department offers more than 300 instruction sessions every year, reaching more than 7,000 students. The library faculty, a team of between eight to ten librarians who actively teach these courses (which are organized and presented in library classrooms each year), are dedicated to finding the most engaging and efficient way to teach library skills to students. The librarians have developed a very strong relationship with various departmental faculty during the many years of teaching, and have a reputation for providing effective, accurate instruction. Issues surrounding human resources and physical space began to have a real impact on the department as the number of incoming students increased. These issues provided motivation to investigate alternative methods of reaching large numbers of students new to the academic library environment.

OBJECTIVES

Hunter College librarians have worked for many years with the college's first-year experience Orientation Seminars (ORSEMs), and this involvement has steadily increased in keeping with growing numbers of incoming students who need to be oriented to the academic library environment. For instance, the Hunter College librarians conducted 226 instruction sessions during the 1992-1993 academic year, teaching about 4,600 students. In 2003-2004, the total number of instruction sessions was 379, reaching more than 7,800 students. This represents an increase of nearly 68 percent. During the summer of 2002, in order to address these concerns, members of the Hunter College reference team began to brainstorm ideas about accomplishing some of the library's instructional goals using an online program. The end result was an online instructional package called VOILA! (http://library.hunter.cuny.edu/orsem/voila.htm) (see Figure C1.1).

One of the primary goals of VOILA! was to prepare first-year students from the ORSEMs for the research orientation they would later receive in foundational English composition courses. VOILA! con-

VOILA!

- Home
- Reference Tutorial
- Virtual Tour
- Call Number Tutorial
- Take the Test
- Help
- Hunter Libraries

Welcome to VOILA!

Welcome to the Hunter College Libraries virtual library orientation, known as "VOILA!". The tutorials are designed to help you familiarize yourself with the Hunter College Libraries environment. You should review each of the tutorials carefully, and feel free to go through them as many times as you'd like. Then, when you are ready, take the test. The test will contain information from each of the three components.

Students new to Hunter may be used to using their public libraries and not academic libraries. How are the Hunter College Libraries different from a public library?

- All books and periodicals are related to Hunter courses.
- The librarians are here to teach the students research skills.

reference tutorial

virtual library tour

call # tutorial

take the test

instructor login

What will you find in Hunter's Library?	What will you usually find in a public library?
• Academic journals • Videos required for class • Music CDs required for class • Scholarly book	• Popular magazines • Current popular videos • Current popular music CDs • The latest bestseller

FIGURE C1.1. The VOILA! Home Page

sists of three tutorials—a call number tutorial based on the Library of Congress system, a reference tutorial focused on using the library's online catalog, a virtual library tour that highlights important collection locations and points of service, and a thirty-two-question quiz. VOILA! was first run as a pilot during the fall 2002 semester. It was a success, but the reference team decided it needed to be improved. Thus began an intense process of review and modification for the program. On the programmatic end, VOILA! became a requirement for all students registered in the ORSEMs, a critical change that highlighted the library as an active and important contributor to the first-year experience program at Hunter College.

Hunter librarians thought it important that the objectives for the VOILA! project be closely tied to the Association of College and Research Libraries (ACRL) standards for information competency. These guidelines provided a foundation for the tutorials, and guided the development of the content. In keeping with the ACRL standards, Hunter librarians determined that students should eventually be able to

- identify library-use concepts by name and function (e.g., services, service desks, the online catalog, and journal-related terms);
- distinguish one material type from another (books, periodicals, reference sources, and microforms);
- recall concepts and rules relating to arrangement of library materials (by Library of Congress call numbers or alphabetical schemes); and
- apply rules related to using the OPAC (simple search construction and item location information in the catalog record).

Aside from the information competencies that VOILA! sought to address, there were programmatic objectives for the program. Achieving a low cost/benefit ratio was an important consideration, as Hunter librarians had to take into account the small number of instructional library staff and limited financial resources available for teaching. A second programmatic objective was to establish the library as an innovator within the Hunter College community, and highlight the library staff's efforts to take advantage of the hypertext environment to provide instruction. This objective was later evidenced in part by a number of contacts made by departments outside of the library seeking the input of librarians involved with VOILA! especially in terms of developing similar methods for delivering information to new students electronically. Another primary objective for the VOILA! team was to become more actively involved in assessment—in particular, evaluation of instructional efforts—to guide future instruction. This led to efforts to evaluate the educational effectiveness and design of both the tutorials and the quiz.

METHODS

Initial Planning and Feasibility Review

The planning and development stages for VOILA! were very important and took place over the course of five months. The development team was made up of librarians and staff from the library's reference department, and this collective was responsible for all aspects of research and development for the project. Specific steps were taken before implementing the pilot program, and this predevelopment stage proved to be extremely useful. The activities during this time period included meeting with other professional staff involved in library instruction and information literacy; meeting with ORSEM program coordinators and instructors; a comprehensive literature and data review of current online instruction practice and methods of delivery for information competency tutorials; examination of previous instructional statistics for the department; review of session and class bookings in the library; and discussing the costs of implementing a new program such as VOILA! The following section highlights the key components for each task:

- Meeting with other professional staff involved in library instruction and information literacy. Involvement of both librarians and other staff who were often in contact with new students was important to the success of the project. Feedback about whether or not an online model would work was solicited and carefully considered.
- A comprehensive literature and data review of current online instruction practice and methods of delivery for information competency tutorials. Literature documenting experiences at other campuses, best practices, and cautions were carefully reviewed. These articles provided a foundation for the project, and were also used to help formulate an initial feasibility statement.
- Examination of previous instructional statistics for the department and review of session and class bookings in the library. The instructional department kept well-organized and up-to-date statistics on the numbers of requests for classes, the type of material taught, the numbers of students taught, the time frame for the classes, and the library location in which the classes were taught. Librarians reviewed these statistics and made decisions accordingly. These statistics highlighted the fact that library space for teaching was at capacity, and alternatives for teaching such large numbers of students had to be found.
- Meeting with ORSEM program coordinators and instructors. These meetings allowed ORSEM program coordinators to provide important information about the nature of the first-year ex-

perience, which in turn helped librarians to focus their efforts and design a program that would be appropriate for the target population.

- Discussion regarding the costs (human and financial) of implementing a new program such as VOILA! Careful consideration was given to the costs of developing and implementing a new program. It was important that the cost-per-instructional-contact be aligned with the departmental goal of providing effective instruction, but also allow librarians to maximize their time and resources. Librarians also had to determine how they would fit in new tasks associated with the development and maintenance of the program with their current responsibilities, such as staffing the reference desk.

Literature Overview

The electronic delivery of VOILA! meant that students could take VOILA! whenever they wanted to, from any computer with an Internet connection. Students normally have about two weeks to complete the tutorials, and then take the test. Prior to implementing VOILA! Hunter librarians reviewed the professional literature to gather information on virtual learning and whether or not an online tutorial would be appropriate for Hunter's ORSEM students. Of particular importance was the effectiveness of the online tutorial as compared to in-class instruction. In a study conducted by Nichols and colleagues at the State University of New York at Oswego, the researchers found that students learned as much from online tutorials as they did from traditional in-class sessions.[1] They analyzed pre- and post-test mean scores for two groups of students, and found no statistical difference in terms of performance. They also looked at student satisfaction with both modes, and found that students were equally as satisfied with online instruction as they were with traditional instruction. Tiefel stresses the importance of utilizing technology to provide library and information instruction, as the Web provides ample opportunity to design online learning tools for a variety of different learning styles.[2] Wegner and colleagues suggest that computer-based instruction is particularly suited to learning how-to skills, such as locating and using information, skills that are certainly in line with VOILA!'s content.[3] Of particular interest to the librarians were the authors' findings that students who attended "live" classroom sessions showed no significant difference when compared with students who participated in virtual sessions with regard to achievement. In findings similar to Nichols and colleagues, Wegner and colleagues found that the virtual group showed a slightly higher rate of satisfaction. Dewald maintains that information provided in small blocks with parts and subparts is easier for students to absorb, stating, "the hypertext landscape was originally designed to allow the user to select their own paths through information, and the best Web-based instructional programs facilitate this as part of an active learning process."[4] Varner and colleagues found that students wanted not only instruction about how to use library resources but the opportunity to experiment with electronic resources such as library databases and library catalogs, at the time of the instruction.[5] In keeping with this, VOILA! provided links to the library catalog, databases, and other resources highlighted in the various instructional modules to allow students to try out what they had just learned. One of the most important features of VOILA! is the complementary design that is meant to intersect with and support future instruction. Dewhurst and Williams agree with the use of online instruction in this way, suggesting that online tutorials are an effective and appropriate supplement to classroom instruction, but not a replacement.[6]

VOILA! Test Construction

The VOILA! test was developed collectively by Hunter librarians. This process was guided by a Hunter librarian with a background in instructional design and assessment. The test was developed in an interactive manner over the course of three years, and this review and modification process yielded a well-thought-out testing instrument. The obvious purpose of the test is to gauge what students have recently learned from the VOILA! tutorials, but the librarians also use this test in a variety of other ways. As a pretest assessment, it provides a glimpse of the areas most confusing to students, allowing librarians to tailor instruction for each class as necessary. Librarians can also share feedback with instructors about student performance and how this might impact future research assignments.

The VOILA! test is an objective instrument comprised of multiple-choice, true-false, matching, fill-in-the-blank, and short-answer questions. The questions reflect material normally presented to incoming students at the ORSEMs, and, also, the types of questions new students tended to ask at the reference desk. The first version of the VOILA! quiz (fall 2002) consisted of forty-two questions, and an estimated 600 students from more than seventy ORSEM sections took the quiz. Feedback from students suggested that the quiz was too long, and in spring 2003, the next version was shortened to thirty-four questions.

The test continued to be revised, and the third version of VOILA! consisting of thirty-two questions was administered during the fall 2003 semester.

Some of the questions with a very high error rate were examined, checked for clarity, and compared with the tutorial content for consistency. During the fall 2003 semester, results were reviewed for problem questions and these questions were rewritten. Two additional questions were added to make sure that adequate coverage of a topic (in this case, screen interpretation for the library catalog, CUNY+) was provided. The fourth version of the VOILA! test (fall 2004) consisted of thirty-two questions, each having been through numerous revisions. Refer to Table C1.1 for quiz results and see the Appendix for a copy of the most recent version of the quiz.

Technology

The Hunter College Library Systems department played a critical role in the development and implementation of VOILA! Librarians consulted systems staff throughout the development process, and worked very closely with them to make sure the project ran smoothly. Effective communication about the goals of the project, technical specifications and details such as the project timeline were central to VOILA!'s success.

Students submitted answers to the first VOILA! test to a Web-based e-mail account. The test itself was created using freeware called Quiz-Test.[7] The software was highly customizable and easy to use, and librarians worked with systems staff to ensure accuracy of data input (see Figure C1.2).

Librarians accessed the account, and printed and scored the tests by hand. Results were sent to instructors via campus mail for them to share with their students. For fall 2003, the quiz was scored electroni-

INBOX Compose Folders Options Search Help Address Book Password Logout   Check Mail Usage   Open Folde

VOILA Quizzes Fall2003   **Page 62 of 62**   **1221 to 1**

Select ▾ Mark as: ▾   ◁ ◁ 62 ▷ ▷   Move | Cop

Delete | Undelete

☑	▲ #	▲ Date	▲ From	▲ Subject [Thread]
☐	17	10/09/03	library.hunter.cuny.edu	ORSEM Library Information Quiz Quiz Results: Dimit...
☐	16	10/09/03	library.hunter.cuny.edu	ORSEM Library Information Quiz Quiz Results: Sara ...
☐	15	10/09/03	library.hunter.cuny.edu	ORSEM Library Information Quiz Quiz Results: Jana ...
☐	14	10/09/03	library.hunter.cuny.edu	ORSEM Library Information Quiz Quiz Results: poprz...
☐	5	10/09/03	library.hunter.cuny.edu	ORSEM Library Information Quiz Quiz Results: jessi...
☐	4	10/09/03	library.hunter.cuny.edu	ORSEM Library Information Quiz Quiz Results: Roxan...
☐	3	10/09/03	library.hunter.cuny.edu	ORSEM Library Information Quiz Quiz Results: nicol...
☐	13	10/09/03	library.hunter.cuny.edu	ORSEM Library Information Quiz Quiz Results: asima ...
☐	12	10/09/03	library.hunter.cuny.edu	ORSEM Library Information Quiz Quiz Results: phili...
☐	11	10/09/03	library.hunter.cuny.edu	ORSEM Library Information Quiz Quiz Results: Karla...
☐	10	10/09/03	library.hunter.cuny.edu	ORSEM Library Information Quiz Quiz Results: Miche...
☐	9	10/09/03	library.hunter.cuny.edu	ORSEM Library Information Quiz Quiz Results: David...
☐	8	10/09/03	library.hunter.cuny.edu	ORSEM Library Information Quiz Quiz Results: Georg...
☐	7*	10/09/03	library.hunter.cuny.edu	ORSEM Library Information Quiz Quiz Results: John ...
☐	6	10/09/03	library.hunter.cuny.edu	ORSEM Library Information Quiz Quiz Results: Sana ...
☐	2	10/09/03	library.hunter.cuny.edu	ORSEM Library Information Quiz Quiz Results: Mats ...
☐	1	10/09/03	library.hunter.cuny.edu	ORSEM Library Information Quiz Quiz Results: Willi...

FIGURE C1.2. The Web-Based E-Mail Account Used to Collect the First VOILA! Test

cally before being forwarded to the e-mail account. The scored tests were then printed and sent to instructors.

The fall 2004 version of the test saw a vast improvement in its administration, which in turn greatly reduced the amount of time spent by librarians collecting, grading, and distributing the tests. Back-end support now includes a homegrown MySQL database designed by the Hunter College systems department (see Figure C1.3).

This new "paperless" system managed the data, collected and sorted the tests, produced statistics (such as average and mean scores) for each section/instructor, and highlighted individual questions that were most and least frequently missed. Instructors could access a results database, searchable by student name or class. Results from the VOILA! test were used by instructors and librarians to more accurately pinpoint weak areas and tailor subsequent instruction accordingly. The database also generated random versions of the test each time a student logged in to take the test, thereby deterring cheating and answer sharing.

VOILA!

Class
Add Class
View Class
Student
View Student
Search Student
Setting
Add User
View User
Tools
Export to SPSS
Quiz Statistics
Sign-Out

Voila Quiz Statistics	
Quiz Version:	Fall 2004
Completed Quizzes:	1353
Number of Classes:	75
Highest Score:	100%
Lowest Score:	28%
Average Score:	78.77%

Quiz V4.x Question Statistics

Most Missed Questions	# Missed		Least Missed Questions	# Missed
Question 29	682		Question 2	21
Question 28	631		Question 16	38
Question 15	558		Question 17	66
Question 25	526		Question 22	85
Question 9	480		Question 18	105

FIGURE C1.3. Descriptive Statistics Displayed in the VOILA! Database

RESULTS

Since its implementation, more than 3,500 students have taken VOILA! The tutorials are reviewed each semester to determine whether or not changes need to be made, based upon student performance; feedback from students, librarians, and instructors; and other factors such as the catalog being modified. Evaluation efforts have included a survey distributed to 600 students soliciting feedback about their VOILA! experience, a review of test validity and reliability, and factor analysis of the test questions. An overview of select test review data is provided in the following section.

General Statistics

In an effort to continuously monitor the performance of students taking VOILA! Hunter librarians tracked results from the VOILA! test starting in the fall 2002 semester, and compiled statistical summaries to present to library staff, program participants, and collaborators outside of the library. The general statistics (see Table C1.1) for the VOILA! test since its inception show a slight increase in the average (mean) scores of the students.

TABLE C1.1. Three-Year Overview of VOILA! Test Statistics

	Fall 2002 N = 158 version 1 42 items	Spring 2003 N = 76 version 2 32 items	Fall 2003 N = 1221 version 2 32 items	Spring 2004 N = 119 version 3 34 items	Fall 2004 N = 1352 version 4 32 items
Highest score	95%	N/A	100%	100%	100%
Lowest score	48%	N/A	.15%	41%	16%
Mean score	71%	N/A	75.91%	78.12%	78.81%
Mode score	67% and 76%	N/A	81.25%	82.35%	88%

Ebel and Frisbie suggest that those designing tests look at statistics to help determine whether the level of difficulty of the test is appropriate for the group being tested.[8] Results from the fall 2003 and fall 2004 VOILA! tests showed that the highest and lowest scores were consistent, but there was a noticeable difference in the mean or average scores. Students who took the test during the fall 2003 semester had a mean score of 75 percent, as compared to the fall 2004 cohort mean score of 79 percent. The test length and the makeup of the student class taking the test remained constant, so other factors such as the modification of problem test items and the related tutorials might account for the significant rise in mean scores.

As VOILA! was a required, graded component of the ORSEMs, instructors had to decide what impact the VOILA! test score would have on the overall course grade for each student. Librarians used descriptive statistics to provide a performance overview for instructors, and provided suggestions for ORSEM instructors with regard to using the scores from the test. One suggestion was for instructors to use the average score for the entire group of students taking the test as a cutoff for a passing grade. The statistics also provided information that the librarians could refer to as they prepared future instruction sessions.

Factor Analysis

One of the unique evaluation methods for the VOILA! test during the fall 2003 and fall 2004 terms was that of a factor analysis. Factor analysis is one method of assessing a test's validity, or whether or not test items are true to the intended purpose of the test. A number of researchers suggest that factor or item analysis is an important tool for evaluating how test questions relate to certain concepts, and Hunter librarians hoped the results of the analysis might shed some light on whether test questions were in keeping with predetermined information competencies. Kline suggests that factor analysis might be used to sort test items into more meaningful groups.[9] Benson and Nasser stress that factor analysis is a way to understand how tests are constructed, and the relationship of test items to broader categories, and to each other.[10] Hunter librarians thought this process would help further their efforts to evaluate the VOILA! test.

SPSS software was used to run the factor analysis, and the analysis produced a five-factor solution, meaning that there were five "factors" or major concepts that the VOILA! test measured. These factors were meaningful to the librarians and proved useful because they provided a statistical overview of the test's content.

CONCLUSION

VOILA! is a virtual library orientation program designed to provide first-year students with the foundation for using the library to conduct basic research. It is now a formal part of the required for-credit orientation seminars at Hunter College. It has been well received and publicized, including conference presentations and a number of academic journal articles. VOILA! is unique in that it was initially developed in house by library staff, with no additional funding. Librarians wrote grant proposals that highlighted the importance and impact of the pilot project, and subsequent grant funding from the college allowed the project to continue to develop. In this way, VOILA! is a model for urban campus libraries with limited funding for special projects, seeking to pilot virtual library instruction and reach large numbers of students effectively. Recent trends in supporting the development of information competencies for all students mean that VOILA! will continue to be evaluated with an eye toward improvement. The success of the project continues to fall heavily on the ability of the development team to communicate and collaborate effectively with departments and professionals outside of the library. Internal administrative backing for the project is also important, and VOILA! has been fully supported by library administration from its inception. The project has provided countless opportunities for those involved on the development side, and tangible results on the user end. Librarians are involved throughout the course of the year with planning meetings for the Hunter College first-year experience program, an unmistakable indication of the importance of information literacy instruction to the college community and the valuable contributions made by librarians. Moreover, the involvement of librarians with such planning in the academic community increases the overall exposure of the library. Future endeavors include continued technological improvements and development of a similar program geared toward graduate students.

APPENDIX: ORSEM LIBRARY INFORMATION QUIZ, FALL 2004, VERSION 4

Instructions

This is an "open book" quiz. Please feel free to refer to your notes, brochures, or handouts from the library, or any material that will help you answer the questions.

Multiple Choice Questions

There is only one correct answer for each question on this quiz. To select an answer, click on the button beside it.

1. The place in the library to go to borrow and return books is called the
   a. Circulation desk
   b. Reserve desk
   c. Reference desk
   d. Periodicals desk
2. For which of these services at Hunter Libraries must you pay cash?
   a. Photocopy cards
   b. Library barcode
   c. Database searching
   d. Internet access
3. It is a good idea to consult a *reference librarian* when you need individual help relating to
   a. Registering for library privileges
   b. Learning advanced features of e-mail
   c. Seeking advice on course selections
   d. Finding term paper or research sources
4. Select the group of titles that you would expect to find in the library's *reference collection*.
   a. Plays, poetry, monologues
   b. Journals, magazines, newsletters
   c. Almanacs, encyclopedias, atlases
   d. Videos, CDs, cassettes
5. In college libraries you will find novels classified and shelved with this collection:
   a. History
   b. Fiction
   c. Literature
   d. Archives

6. Which of these classification numbers follows the system used by the CUNY libraries?
   a. DT 12 .F7 1969
   b. 960.23 Ka6
   c. 557.3 s-dc21
   d. INV. 11552
7. In CUNY college libraries, books about famous people are shelved
   a. By the historical time period in which they lived
   b. In a separate section containing only biographies
   c. On the floor with the B through BX call numbers
   d. Under the subject in which that person is known
8. In most libraries, the computer system you use to search for a book is called the online
   a. Directory
   b. Catalog
   c. Index
   d. Database
9. The City University of New York libraries refer to their search system as:
   a. CUNYSys
   b. CUNYWeb
   c. CUNYInfo
   d. CUNYPlus
10. Below is a search results screen with the title *Concepts of Modern Art* listed on Line 1 and Line 2.

▼ For full record, click line number or title.		▼ To change sort order, click underlined column heading.			▼ For call no., click library name.
#	**Author**	**Title**	**Year**	**Format**	**Holdings**
❯ 1	☐ Stangos, Nikos.	Concepts of modern art.	1998	Book	Hunter-Reserve
❯ 2	☐ Richardson, Tony.	Concepts of modern art.	1974	Book	Hunter-Main

Using the information on the screen, which of these statements is true?
   a. The titles on both Line 1 and Line 2 are the same book.
   b. The title on Line 1 may be used for only two hours.
   c. The title on Line 2 is actually a collection of journals.
   d. The titles on Line 1 and Line 2 are both new books.
11. For which of these books on AIDS would you *have to go* to a Hunter branch library?
   a. *HIV, AIDS, and the Law*
   b. *AIDS Law Today*
   c. *AIDS and Ethics*
   d. *AIDS: Testing and Privacy*

▼ For full record, click line number or title.	▼ To change sort order, click underlined column heading.			▼ For call no., click library name.	
#	Author	Title	Year	Format	Holdings
▷ 1 ☐ Dickson, Donald T.	HIV, AIDS, and the law	2001	Book	Hunter-Social-Work	
▷ 2 ☐ Burris, Scott.	AIDS law today	1993	Book	Hunter-Main	
▷ 3 ☐ Reamer, Frederic	AIDS and ethics /	1991	Book	Hunter-Health-Professions Hunter-Main Hunter-Social-Work	
▷ 4 ☐ Gunderson, Martin	AIDS : testing and privacy /	1989	Book	Hunter-Main Hunter-Social-Work	

12. To find books by the author Richard Ford, you would type in his name like this: _____

13. To find a book called *The Right Stuff,* you would type in: _____

14. In the space below, show how you would enter a search for books on the topic "hunger among the homeless": _____

15. In Hunter Libraries, periodicals are arranged
    a. First by year, then in alphabetical order by title
    b. First by subject, then in alphabetical order by title
    c. First in alphabetical order by title, then by year
    d. First by year, then in alphabetical order by subject

Match the letters beside each line of the call number label in the picture below to the descriptions in questions 16-19.

John Selby

The American Revolution In Virginia

```
E    ——— = A.
203  ———  = B.
.V8  ——— C.
S45  ——— D.
2002
```

16.	Author code	A	B	C	D
17.	Narrow subject	A	B	C	D
18.	Decimal category	A	B	C	D
19.	Broad subject	A	B	C	D

20. When magazines and journals first arrive in the Hunter Libraries, they are shelved in a section called
    a. Periodicals Bound
    b. New Periodicals
    c. Periodical Reserves
    d. Current Periodicals
21. Select the correct alphabetical arrangement for these four magazine titles in the order you would find them on the periodical shelves in Hunter Libraries: _____
    a. *The Shakespeare Newsletter, Social Policy, Teaching K-8, Theater*
    b. *Social Policy, Teaching K-8, The Shakespeare Newsletter, Theater*
    c. *The Shakespeare Newsletter, Social Policy, Theater, Teaching K-8*
    d. *Social Policy, Theater, Teaching K-8, The Shakespeare Newsletter*
22. Which one of these items is considered a library periodical?
    a. Dictionaries
    b. Web sites
    c. Journals
    d. Reserves
23. What is a reference that looks like the one below called?
    Kelker, Katharin A. School services for drug-addicted children. *Preventing School Failure*, Spring 1990, Vol. 34 Issue 3, pp. 22-25.
    a. An entry
    b. A citation
    c. An abstract
    d. A record
24. *Preventing School Failure* in this example refers to:

    a. A book
    b. A journal
    c. An index
    d. An encyclopedia

True-False

Instructions: Click on the button beside the response of your choice.

25. T F In the LC call number, F 3553 .K9 1995, the letter "F" stands for Fiction.
26. T F You can assume that five books all starting with the call number RA 644.A25 are about the same subject.
27. T F The call number QA 761.15 D526 comes *before* the call number QA 76 .765 E95
28. T F In Hunter Libraries, the biography of an author is shelved in the same section as the books written by that author.
29. T F Hunter Libraries use call numbers on books *and* journals.
30. T F Journals from the Hunter Libraries circulate on weekdays after 5 p.m. and must be returned the next day before 9 a.m.
31. T F A *bound* journal is a volume containing two or more consecutive issues.
32. T F To find the journal called *The Clearinghouse,* look on the shelf under *C* for *Clearinghouse.*

NOTES

1. Nichols, J., Shaffer, B., and Shockey, K. Changing the Face of Instruction: Is Online or In-Class More Effective? *College & Research Libraries* 64(5) (2003): 378-388.

2. Tiefel, V.M. Library User Education: Examining Its Past, Projecting Its Future. *Library Trends* 44(2) (1995): 318-338.

3. Wegner, S.B., Holloway, K.C., and Garton, E.M. The Effects of Internet-Based Instruction on Student Learning. *Journal of Asynchronous Learning Networks* 3(2) (1999): 98-106.

4. Dewald, N.H. Web-Based Library Instruction: What Is Good Pedagogy? *Information Technology and Libraries* 18(1) (1999): 26-31.

5. Varner, C.H., Schwartz, V.M., and George, J. Library Instruction and Technology in a General Education "Gateway" Course: The Student's View at Illinois State University. *Journal of Academic Librarianship* 22(5) (1996): 355-359.

6. Dewhurst, D.B. and Williams, A.D. An Investigation of the Potential for a Computer-Based Tutorial Program Covering the Cardiovascular System to Replace Traditional Lectures. *Computers & Education* 31(3) (1998): 301-317.

7. QuizTest v. 3.0, Copyright 1996, Kristina Pfaff-Harris, Reno, Nevada. Available at http://www.tesol.net/scripts/QuizTest. Accessed August 1, 2005.

8. Ebel, Robert and Frisbie, David. *Essentials of Educational Measurement.* Englewood Cliffs, NJ: Prentice Hall, 1986.

9. Kline, Paul. *An Easy Guide to Factor Analysis.* New York: Routledge, 1994.

10. Benson, J. and Nasser, F. On the Use of Factor Analysis As a Research Tool. *Journal of Vocational Education Research* 23(1) (1998): 13-33.

EXERCISES

1. Summarize this case study, stating the main points for a classmate or co-worker who knows very little about the subject or who has not read the case study. Relate this case study to your experience as a student, employee, or customer.

2. Rewrite the summary for a different audience (e.g., expert in the field, college administrator, fund-raiser).

3. With a classmate or co-worker, role-play the case study, with one person playing the author, and the other person asking the author about his or her purpose, motivations, main points, evidence, conclusions, etc.

4. Do you agree or disagree with the main points of the case study? Do you base this on prior knowledge, opinion, author's arguments, cited evidence, intuition, or a combination of these elements?

5. Find two scholarly, authoritative sources (books or articles) that support or refute the main points of this case study. Detail the sources consulted and the search terms used.

6. Based on the evidence presented in the preceding case study, what do you think are the most significant challenges facing academic librarians involved with first-year experience programs for college students?

7. Develop three to five interview questions that could be used to interview a practicing academic librarian about his or her experience providing instruction and reference assistance to students enrolled in a first-year experience course.

8. Write a one-page memorandum to a hypothetical library supervisor justifying why a specific academic library should or should not work closely with teaching faculty to support first-year experience coursework.

Case Study 2

Reference Triage at the Medical University of Ohio: Just-in-Case to Just-in-Time at the Mulford Library

Marlene A. Porter
Jolene M. Miller

INTRODUCTION

As far back as 1876, functions of reference have been identified and discussed in the literature: answering patrons' questions, helping them select appropriate resources, teaching them how to use the library, and promoting the library in the community it serves.[1] Although resource formats and organizational structures have changed over the years, these basic reference functions have not. The relative importance of each of these functions varies among libraries (the reference department at an undergraduate academic library focuses more on the instructional functions, while reference in a library serving a corporation focuses more on providing answers), as well as within a particular library (faculty members may received differing levels of service than students). Variations in relative importance of these functions have resulted in debates over whether libraries should follow the minimal model (also referred to as the conservative model), in which instruction takes a higher priority than providing information, or the maximal model (also referred to as the liberal model), in which provision of information is more important than instruction. Most libraries follow the *via media,* the middle way, providing both instruction and information depending upon the situation.[2]

An Introduction to Reference Services in Academic Libraries
© 2006 by The Haworth Press, Inc. All rights reserved.
doi:10.1300/5634_02

Ultimately, where a library falls on this continuum of reference service depends upon the mission of the institution it serves and the needs of its patrons. Libraries that serve academic medical centers, by their very nature, fall into the *via media,* serving the educational, research, and health care missions of the institution. An academic medical center is a teaching hospital that is affiliated with a medical school. Some centers consist of multiple hospitals, outpatient facilities, and schools of medicine, nursing, pharmacy, allied health, etc. Reference librarians at academic medical center libraries often provide instruction to support the students' classroom education and their development of skills for lifelong learning, while providing information in support of patient care and research. There can be a great deal of flexibility, however, by providing information for students and providing instruction for clinicians and researchers.

Reference service in libraries can be described by characteristics other than position on the minimal-maximal service continuum. For example, how many service desks are there? If there are multiple desks, does each desk provide different types and levels of assistance? How are reference librarians available to their library users— do they sit and wait at a desk? Do librarians wander around the library? Do librarians wander the halls of academic departments? Are librarians available by appointment, phone, e-mail, or chat? In 2001, Fritch and Mandernack published an overview of models of reference services and proposed a new reference paradigm in light of cultural and information changes.[3] They emphasized that while changes in information technology and library users may warrant changes in how reference assistance is provided, planning and management strategies must be based in "thoughtful consideration of our roles within the context of our institutions, our communities, and the larger society."[4] Throughout the transitions in reference service at the Mulford Library, the guiding principle was and continues to be how to best support users (and by extension, the institution and the broader community) in their work, whether learning, caring for patients, or doing research.

SETTING

The Medical University of Ohio (MUO) is an academic medical center in northwest Ohio. It includes schools of medicine, nursing, and allied health, three teaching hospitals (acute medical care, psychiatric, and rehabilitation), and a variety of outpatient clinics. MUO's Mulford Library serves a diverse clientele: students, clinical and non-clinical staff members, resident physicians, and clinical and research faculty, as well as patients, family members, and other members of the community. Students represent a wide range of disciplines in clinical care and research. Over 550 students are enrolled in the traditional four-year MD program, with an additional ten students enrolled in the seven-year MD/PhD program. Over 200 resident physicians in sixteen graduate medical education programs are served by the library. Doctoral and master's degrees are granted in the basic sciences (biochemistry, cancer biology, neuroanatomy, radiation/medical physics, etc.). Undergraduate nursing students from two neighboring universities come to MUO for their clinical education, and graduate programs include clinical nurse specialist and family and pediatric nurse practitioner, as well as an entry-level master's level program for people with nonnursing bachelor's degrees. Allied health programs (physician assistant, occupational and physical therapy, and public and occupational health) are all graduate-level programs with an emphasis on research as well as clinical competencies.

In addition to serving students, the library also provides information support for staff and faculty in patient care and hospital administration. Support for clinical and basic sciences research range: from literature searches for grants and Institutional Review Board (for the protection of human research subjects) applications, to searching for statistical data and providing support for bibliographic management software. In addition to the primary clientele of faculty, residents, staff, and students, Mulford Library also provides information services to the wider community. Patients and their family members often seek information on a newly diagnosed disease, local high school and undergraduate students request information for class assignments, and local law offices need information for cases.

MUO is a member of the Ohio Library and Information Network (OhioLINK), the consortium of Ohio's college, university, and research libraries: seventeen public universities, twenty-three community/technical colleges, forty-four private colleges, and the State Library of Ohio. OhioLINK offers six main electronic services: a library catalog, research databases, a multi-publisher electronic journal center, a digital media center, a growing collection of online books, and an electronic theses and dissertations center. In 2003, OhioLINK launched a statewide cooperative chat reference service that included Mulford Library participation from the beginning. In 2004, using OhioLINK's chat software, health sciences librarians began offering a chat reference service specifically for health sciences questions, again including Mulford Library participation.

Mulford Library's Information Services (IS) Department encompasses reference and instructional services. IS staff members include the department head, the reference/education librarian (who coordinates the educational efforts of the library in addition to providing reference assistance), a part-time reference librarian, and a full-time reference associate. In addition, two librarians outside of the IS department, the associate director for library services and the digital services librarian, spend some time each week providing reference assistance.

OBJECTIVE

With dwindling traffic at the reference desk, IS librarians sought better ways to provide reference assistance than the traditional "librarian-waiting-at-a-desk" model.[5] The new model of reference assistance, introduced in September 2004, is multifaceted: just-in-time reference triage at the circulation desk for in-person patrons, use of chat reference and consultation appointments, as well as maintenance of previously established systems of telephone and e-mail reference. A number of factors influenced our decision to move to a triage or tiered approach to reference, primarily changes in library use and changes in librarian responsibilities.

First, there have been significant changes in library use, with fewer people coming into the library for reference help. The number of transactions at the reference desk declined 32 percent over the past five years. In addition to the overall decline in reference activity, reference librarians reported anecdotally that they received increasing numbers of questions by phone and e-mail, and fewer in-person requests. This can be partially attributed to the wider availability of online resources. Faculty, staff, and students have off-campus access to all of the library's databases, and to nearly all of the online full-text books, journals, and clinical resources such as UpToDate. When they have questions, they pick up the phone to call rather than coming to the library. The decrease in reference questions may be due to students being skilled enough to find information that is roughly what they need and being willing to accept it, even though it is not useful for their assignment or project.[6] Unfortunately, this may also be true for faculty members. Statistics also suggest that questions generally fit into two distinctive groups: quick questions (how to access/do you have item) and in-depth research questions. Based on the experience of providing assistance with bibliographic management software with office visits, librarians also began to offer increasing numbers of reference consultations for users with in-depth reference or instructional issues.

In addition to the changes in the amount and mix of transactions at the reference desk, librarian workload has increased as well. In fiscal year 2005, the library eliminated a professional position in the IS department, which directly reduced the number of available staff hours, and indirectly shifted librarian teaching loads. Under the traditional model, the eliminated position covered over 110 hours of reference staffing time and over 30 hours of instruction annually. In addition, the two full-time librarians in the department have faculty status, which entails research and service responsibilities, such as work for institutional, OhioLINK, and professional association committees. These librarians provide much of the instruction for the library's information management elective for fourth-year medical students and have additional responsibilities to the departments in which they have their faculty appointments, such as participating in the student admissions process and advising students on scholarly projects.[7] Eliminating the reference desk allowed the IS staff to work more efficiently and effectively, at their own desks and computers, without being interrupted by routine questions such as where the restrooms are located.

METHODS

Planning

Once the need for a different model of reference service was identified, the assistant director for library services, head of information services, and head of access services (who supervises the circulation desk) began meeting regularly to discuss the possibilities. The initial planning process included reviewing reference desk interaction statistics and reviewing the literature to determine how other institutions eliminated reference desks, consolidated service desks, or utilized paraprofessionals to answer reference questions. Discussions culminated with a plan to eliminate the reference desk in favor of reference triage, a tiered reference model with the circulation desk staff members receiving the questions, addressing those they could answer while passing the more complex or difficult questions on to a librarian.[8]

Based on this information, the head of information services wrote a proposal outlining actions to be taken to move from the just-in-case reference desk to just-in-time reference services. Issues addressed in the proposal included developing policies and training for circulation staff members in handling questions, developing chat reference training for two IS department staff members, determining when reference librarians would be available and how they would be available (backup, chat, and consultations), developing new forms of online educational material (for use by library users and library staff alike), as well as more practical tasks such as determining where the reference desk phone, computer, and other resources would be relocated. The plan for replacing the reference desk with these alternative forms of reference assistance was proposed in May 2004, with a transition process to occur over about four months. Because the Mulford Library is a relatively small library, the transition was achieved in four months. A larger library would need additional time.

Transitioning

Closing the reference desk required training of the circulation desk staff. Held the month before the transition to one desk, training sessions included how to handle reference questions, including when to refer; using MEDLINE and other commonly used databases; and chat reference basics so they would feel comfortable referring people to the chat service. To minimize staff anxiety surrounding the change, training repeatedly emphasized that desk staff should not feel inadequate about being unable to answer all questions and not be afraid to refer users to a reference librarian. The library's reference help Web page was revised and updated to include links to chat, request forms, and other information for assisting users. A consultation Web form was also created to give users the option of scheduling a time to meet with a librarian. In addition to modifying existing Web pages, the library purchased Camtasia, a software product for creating online tutorials for use when reference assistance is not available. These online tutorials can also be used as refreshers by circulation desk staff members. Moving the reference desk computer and telephone was facilitated by staff downsizing that occurred during the transition. An office in the information services area was vacated, and the reference computer and telephone were moved to the office. This gave the IS staff an area for consultation, the creation and testing of online tutorials, and a meeting area.

Scheduling

Reference desk statistics for five years were reviewed to determine when different types of questions (technical, quick, in-depth, educational, etc.) commonly occurred; this information was used to determine the initial reference services schedule. Reference backup for the circulation desk took two forms: in-person backup and chat reference. Reference backup is available Monday through Friday, 10:00 a.m. to 5:00 p.m. When a librarian is on backup, he or she handles telephone calls to the old reference desk phone number, as well as handling questions referred from the circulation desk. All staff members that previously staffed the reference desk are scheduled for in-person backup on a regular schedule, with regularly assigned shifts of three to four hours each week.

Because of previous experience with the OhioLINK chat reference service, most of the IS staff members were familiar with chat reference and the chat software. Two staff members were new to chat and required training, which was developed and implemented by the reference/education librarian, and involved hands-on training, chat practice with experienced librarians, and peer review of chat transcripts. Training occurred approximately one month before the transition was made. Local chat reference services are available Monday through Friday, from 10:00 a.m. to 12:00 p.m. and from 1:00 to 5:00 p.m. Because Mulford librarians also help staff the OhioLINK general chat reference service and the OhioLINK health sciences chat reference service, they staff the OhioLINK services at times that are best for their local users: Sundays from 1:00 to 5:00 p.m., and Tuesdays from 6:00 to 9:00 p.m. Mulford librarians are on chat reference thirty-seven hours per week. In addition to these hours, users have access to statewide chat reference service through OhioLINK and KnowItNow 24/7, another Ohio-based chat reference service. These services are available not only to patrons but also to library staff members. If a circulation desk staff member needs help with a reference question when a Mulford librarian is not available, help is available on one of the other chat services.

Marketing

Marketing of the reference desk closing and availability of the new chat and consultation services was accomplished several ways including campus-wide flyers, e-mail messages sent to all library staff and campus faculty, via the campus news service and in training sessions librarians participated in. Announcements were also made at campus committee meetings and in departments that have affiliated librarians with faculty status. Marketing needs to be an ongoing process.

Evaluation

The evaluation plan of this new model of reference service is multifaceted. Standard reference statistics are collected for all local services—circulation desk, reference backup, and chat—as a way to determine how use changes over time. Mulford librarians currently use paper forms, but a Web-based statistics form is being developed to automate and consolidate the process as well as enable the library to better analyze service use. Assessments of staff member attitudes were planned for spring 2005 semester to determine their feelings about the new model.

RESULTS

Transitioning from a just-in-case reference model to a just-in-time model was generally smooth. There were some minor hiccups in the beginning, mostly logistical, though some were compounded by staff anxiety. One such example was determining to which telephone the reference assistance telephone calls would be forwarded. Initially, reference assistance calls were going to be transferred to the circulation desk, but when circulation staff complained, it was decided that the telephone would be forwarded to whoever was scheduled on backup, and to voice mail when a librarian was not on backup. This has worked well and, as an added benefit, the circulation staff need only dial the reference assistance number to contact whoever is scheduled for backup. The transition was not as major as it initially appeared because it is based on a subtle yet existing reference model. In the old model, the circulation desk was far more visible and convenient for users. Circulation desk staff often received reference questions beyond their ability to answer. In these cases, they would refer the user to the reference desk (if staffed) or call a librarian who was in his or her office. The new model streamlines the reference process: one desk at which to stop, with expert assistance on call, if needed.

Lessons Learned

Important factors for making a smooth transition to triage reference include authority, cooperation, buy-in, and communication by all involved. One person needs to coordinate the whole effort and have authority over the whole process. It was difficult with two department heads involved, but only one made most of the decisions and coordinated the whole effort. Also, staff needs reassurance that they will be supported in the event they are overwhelmed with users.

Marketing and patience are necessary in making the service work. Constant marketing of chat and consultation is needed to reach all possible users. As noted previously, marketing is an ongoing process.

As of this writing, the transition to one service desk is working well. Continual adjustments have been made such as combining chat and reference backup during the Monday through Friday mornings and Friday afternoons when there is less activity. More and creative marketing will be done concerning chat and consultation. Chat and consultation will continue to be marketed to students in classroom settings, faculty in departmental meetings, and both groups by e-mail.

NOTES

1. Tyckoson, David A. What Is the Best Model of Reference Service? *Library Trends* 50(Fall) (2001) 183-196.
2. Ibid.
3. Fritch, John W. and Mandernack, Scott B. The Emerging Reference Paradigm: A Vision of Reference Services in a Complex Information Environment. *Library Trends* 50(Fall) (2001) 286-305.
4. Ibid.
5. Lipow, Anne Grodzins. The Future of Reference: Point-of-Need Reference Service: No Longer an Afterthought. *Reference Services Review* 31(1) (2003): 31-35.
6. Troll, Denise A. How and Why Libraries Are Changing: What We Know and What We Need to Know. *Portal: Libraries and the Academy* 2(1) (2002): 99-123.
7. Miller, Jolene M. Issues Surrounding the Administration of a Credit Course for Medical Students: Survey of US Academic Health Sciences Librarians. *Journal of the Medical Library Association* 92(July) (2004): 354-363.
8. Graves, Karen J. Implementation and Evaluation of Information Desk Services Provided by Library Technical Assistants. *Bulletin of the Medical Library Association* 86(October) (1998): 475-485.

EXERCISES

1. Summarize this case study, stating the main points for a classmate or co-worker who knows very little about the subject or who has not read the case study. Relate this case study to your experience as a student, employee, or customer.
2. Rewrite the summary for a different audience (expert in the field, college administrator, fund-raiser).
3. With a classmate or co-worker, role-play the case study, with one person playing the author, and the other person asking the author about his or her purpose, motivations, main points, evidence, conclusions, etc.
4. Do you agree or disagree with the main points of the case study? Do you base this on prior knowledge, opinion, authors' arguments, cited evidence, intuition, or a combination of these elements?
5. Find two scholarly, authoritative sources (books or articles) that support or refute the main points of this case study. Detail the sources consulted and the search terms used.
6. Based on the evidence presented in the preceding case study, what do you think are the most significant challenges facing academic librarians choosing to reduce or combine service points?

7. Develop three to five interview questions that could be used to interview a practicing academic librarian about his or her experience using reference triage.
8. Write a one-page memorandum explaining the concept of reference triage and why it should or should not be implemented in a specific academic library setting.

Case Study 3

Marketing Library Services to Young Male Faculty

Mary Mee

INTRODUCTION

Every small college library, especially those isolated from metropolitan advantages, where local economies are based on heavy agriculture and light manufacturing, struggles to market its services to young male faculty. Such faculty are in short supply and librarians must work to attract them to all the library has to offer: its knowledge resources, calm demeanor, and mature charm. This study follows three strategies tried by the Fraught Memorial Library during the fall 2003 and spring 2004 semesters.

STRATEGIES

Strategy One: Dress Up the Library— From Frumpy to Sophisticated

The library set out to create a more attractive environment. Though funding for a full face-lift was not available, staff recognized several areas for low-cost improvements. Before the beginning of the semester, staff volunteered free time to dust and scrub the neglected corners of the library, areas that had seen very little activity for several years; gave the face and entry of the library a new coat of paint, nothing garish, but enough to hide the signs of age; and to laid down a new carpet of a slightly lighter color.

An Introduction to Reference Services in Academic Libraries
© 2006 by The Haworth Press, Inc. All rights reserved.
doi:10.1300/5634_03

Results

Although several assistant professors were heard to remark on the sudden attractiveness of the library, none bothered to actually approach. Staff developed several theories to explain this result. Some said the target faculty were completely satisfied by the information they find on the Internet and were not sufficiently curious to seek and find the superior information that a real library can offer. Others speculated that perhaps the current crop of young male faculty gathered information from one another and had no interest in libraries, and were in fact born that way and there was nothing one could do about it.

Strategy Two: Bait and Switch

Librarians sought to refresh the monograph collection in areas of interest to the young male faculty, then target market those new resources. Staff studied the problem and realized that the faculty in question were primarily from three fields: European history, early-twentieth-century American literature, and geology. Librarians then scoured the marketplace for new monographs in those fields and submitted their requests to the Acquisitions Section. Once purchased, the librarians chose to directly market the new products by slipping suggestive bibliographies under the office doors of the target faculty.

Results

Unfortunately, the "buying spree" corresponded with a new directive to emphasize electronic resources. About 84 percent of the requested monographs were purchased as e-books and the frustrated librarians saw no marked increase in traffic from the objects of their pursuit. Several librarians decided to cease all communication with acquisitions staff.

Strategy Three: Special Programs

A committee of librarians, still hoping for success and still yearning for increased interaction with the target audience, met informally to develop a series of special programs sure to attract. Initial suggestions for "Night Club Night" and "Auto Show Weekend" were dismissed by the library director as "desperate seeming." The two approved special events were a visit from Brett Favre, quarterback for the Green Bay Packers, who would read aloud from his current contract; and a campus tech show featuring new gadgets loosely associated with "information technology."

Results

The Brett Favre reading, though it drew much attention from the fraternities, was poorly attended by the target demographic, prompting a resurgence of speculation that said faculty were not the type of men interested in sports, contracts, or any sort of heroic pursuit, and that, in fact, the librarians were better off without them.

The tech show, however, finally delivered the intended audience. Library staff were very excited by the turnout until it became clear that the young male faculty were too focused on the display of gadgets and devices to appreciate the beauty and sophistication of the library environment. Ironically, the strategy that appeared to be the most effective was actually the most demoralizing.

CONCLUSION

Although marketing library services should not be discouraged, specific audiences, however desirable, will not be drawn into discourse and will not explore their information options. For the sake of library morale, the better approach may be to accept this shortfall and encourage the staff to compensate through yoga, frequent trips to Greece, or cat ownership.

EXERCISES

1. Summarize this case study, stating the main points for a classmate or co-worker who knows very little about the subject or who has not read the case study. Relate this case study to your experience as a student, employee, or customer.
2. Rewrite the summary for a different audience (expert in the field, college administrator, fund-raiser).

3. With a classmate or co-worker, role-play the case study, with one person playing the author, and the other person asking the author about his or her purpose, motivations, main points, evidence, conclusions, etc.

4. Do you agree or disagree with the main points of the case study? Do you base this on prior knowledge, opinion, author's arguments, cited evidence, intuition, or a combination of these elements? Does humor help highlight important concepts?

5. Find two scholarly, authoritative sources (books or articles) that support or refute the main points of this case study. Detail the sources consulted and the search terms used.

6. Based on the evidence presented in the preceding case study, what do you think are the most significant challenges facing academic librarians interested in marketing library services to different segments of the campus community?

7. Develop three to five interview questions that could be used to interview a practicing academic librarian about his or her experience marketing library services to different segments of the campus community.

8. Write a one-page memorandum to a hypothetical college administrator justifying why a specific academic library should or should not be involved in the planning and implementation of online learning.

Case Study 4

Relational Reference: A Challenge to the Reference Fortress

John E. Holberg

Walk into most academic libraries and behold the reference for-
tress from which the librarian ensconced on a dais or entrenched behind a gigantic desk (which provides no personal place of connecting
for a student, faculty member, or patron) interrogates customers and
metes out products. Many librarians have seen and worked at this for-
tress while talking about accessibility, about connecting, and about
an ethic of service instead atmospherically project a lack of interest,
an attitude of unapproachability, and a posture of distancing. It is not
that librarians are not cognizant of these challenges to accessibility
and to perceptions of remoteness, nor is it the case that individuals
have not thought about remedies to issues of space, the library environment, and user services.

Writing in 1992, Virginia Massey-Burzio summarized a number of
deficiencies in reference services, as noted in the literature. For one,
taking note of Friedes, Massey-Burzio states that "the reference desk
can actually act more as an impediment than a facilitator to high-
quality assistance because users perceive it as intended for simple
questions and quick replies."[1] Second, that although there exist "lively
discussions going on about the quality of reference service and how
reference librarians should be spending their time, few analyze or
question how the environment of the reference desk affects the reference encounter."[2] Third, referencing the findings of Durrance, Massey-
Burzio affirms that "our current reference setting makes it difficult

An Introduction to Reference Services in Academic Libraries
© 2006 by The Haworth Press, Inc. All rights reserved.
doi:10.1300/5634_04

for library users to establish a relationship with someone in the library, to work with one person in an ongoing way, and to discuss information needs in depth."[3] Fourth, to remedy these deficiencies libraries must "change the environment."[4]

Since the writing of Massey-Burzio's article a number of substantial changes have occurred within libraries. In recent years, new approaches to reference service have arisen—24/7 service via electronic devices, tiered reference, roving, campus outreach programs, and the like. In some instances, individuals have even heeded the necessity to "change the environment." One such environmental change has been to focus upon the needs of students by installing "dual monitors" at the reference desk, "one facing the patron and the other facing the reference staff."[5] Debates continue to rage about the merits and demerits of the desk versus the counter in creating the appropriate space.[6] Although much of the recent literature on reference services has shifted to examine the larger issues of disintermediation and of disembodied reference work provided via technologies, the desk/ counter remains ubiquitous, and the issue remains unresolved as to how to best reach the students, faculty, and others who physically constitute the embodied community.

Rieh notes

> considering that the essence of reference service is the interaction process between librarians and users, alternative reference service models can best be redesigned by looking more closely at how users are dealing with information problems and how they get help from reference librarians in technological environments.[7]

Just as librarians are expending much thought on virtual reference, so there exists an equally pressing need to refocus attention on space and being issues within physical reference. Spaces and a sense of place must be created that affirm the profession's expression of service and accessibility. What follows is a case study that links theory and praxis in a simple redesign of the reference space for a small liberal arts college in order to address the access difficulties of high-quality and in-depth personal research assistance as well as the effect of the environment on reference.

RELATIONAL REFERENCE

The impulse to change the face of services at The Kresge Memorial Library of Covenant College began in the summer of 2002 with alterations to the space and organization of the periodical back-issues room; with furniture arrangement; and with the addition of signage, cantilever shelving in the current periodicals section, and a new book display on the ground floor. For a number of years prior to 2002, reference had been performed from an office, with no service-point located on the floor. Thus, a reference desk was added for a better sense of approachability. The head librarian wanted to adjust both the sense of accessibility to reference services and to enhance the library's relationship with the wider campus. On the whole, Covenant College's wider campus possesses an ethic of individual attention in instruction, of personal development in tandem with a resolute commitment toward community service, and of the community as a place of being. The librarians at Kresge sought to take into account, to replicate, and even to enhance this campus ecology of individual attention as embedded within a community in the library's reference services. As Tyckoson points out, "in determining the best model [of reference] for a specific library, the values of the community that the library serves must be taken into account."[8] For two years reference services were performed from a traditional reference desk on the floor (as well as with roving), yet the reference space and the setup of the desk had not matched the current reference librarian's desire of interaction with students based upon collaboration in the reference process. There still existed too much spatial disruption from the arm of the desk, which placed the user on one side of the desk and the librarian on the other and confined viewing the computer's screen merely to the reference librarian.

In the summer of 2004, The Kresge Memorial Library moved to continue to make changes to space and to address issues of being within the library, which reflected the vision of the library and the wider campus. This vision emphasizes a strong sense of affirming, individualized, and service-oriented user services—which builds upon what will be termed here relational reference (personal relationships with students and with faculty, built both within the library and within the general setting of the college). In an extremely instructive article Harley, Dreger, and Knobloch note that "academic librarians should adopt as their primary goal enhancing interaction with students."[9] By being involved in campus activities, by knowing the student holistically within the wider interactions of the campus community, and by seeing his or her life not just as a single-faceted hit-and-run encounter at the reference desk, the librarians at Kresge are able to customize their help by working within the context of existing relationships. As Huwe writes, "relationships determine success, and knowledge work is all about relationships."[10] This is not merely about capitalizing upon some slogan or upon some novel technique designed to get more patrons or customers or whatever; rather, it is about creating real relationships with others, serving them more effectively, and promoting the conditions for a community of learning.

REFERENCE AS BEING

In promoting the conditions for a community of learning, relational reference is a way of being that replicates the individual attention and connecting in the classroom setting by providing individualized reference: face-to-face, rapport-based, and collaborative—not merely ready reference but rather research reference. It is not consumerist (which objectifies information and the user), and it is not authoritarian in impulse. Just as other disciplines within the college seek to know and cultivate their students, the library as a discipline and as a community seeks to know its students. Just as disciplines do not merely teach the "facts" or the "know-what" of their disciplines but also the way of being part of the discipline or the "know-how" so the reference encounter is designed to enculturate the user into a way of being a researcher—into the spontaneous habits of the search. According to Wilder, "students are apprentices in the reading and writing of their chosen disciplines, and librarians are experts who can help them master those tasks."[11] Relational reference helps to promote a particular knowledge set (explicit knowledge), as well as a way of being (tacit knowledge). As Brown states, "knowledge has two dimensions, the explicit and tacit. The explicit dimension deals with concepts—the "know-*whats*"—whereas the tacit deals with "know-*how*," which is best manifested in work practices and skills."[12] This knowing happens in a community of doing. Brown continues this line of thinking by stating that "learning to learn happens most naturally when you and a participant are situated in a community of practice . . . recall that [learning] always involves processes of enculturation. Enculturation lies at the heart of learning."[13] Indeed, this idea of enculturation is not particularly novel in small, liberal arts settings nor is it unusual in libraries. Ideally, life at a small liberal arts college works organically to build community and a particular culture; librarians may see a particular student on the playing field in one hour, creating art two hours later, or researching a project in the evening. What may be novel though is how the librarians at Kresge have come to use space and technologies to achieve their community of learning—their "community of practice."

COMMUNITY OF PRACTICE

In moving to foster a "community of practice" for research, the reference librarian at Kresge Memorial Library, in the summer of 2004, restructured his service area to allow for access, for individual attention, and for maximum collaboration between the librarian and a student. As opposed to the traditional counter or desk, he created a reference table—six feet long with two padded, rocking chairs (Sauder PlyLok Series) placed side by side, with a flat-screen monitor on the desktop, and with the CPU mounted unobtrusively beneath the desk. This six-foot-long table looks much like the reading tables in the space—thereby reducing unnecessary hierarchies in which as suggested by Harley, Dreger, and Knobloch: "students can prefer to avoid contact with perceived authority figures."[14]

It might be helpful in this context to think of research librarians simply as more advanced students—with highly developed disciplinary skills of research—and as the endeavor of research as a collaboration between a junior and senior member of college. As Donham and Green conclude, within their consultative model of librarianship, "students began to view librarians not only as specialists, but also collaborators, there to help support students' intellectual endeavors."[15] Just as librarians have a body of expertise, it may serve them well to remember to value and respect the knowledge that each individual student, as well as any patron, also brings to the process.

Aside from minimizing rigid and possibly ominous obstacles to access, the space itself promotes a number of additional objectives. First, it creates a space for the patron in the research process. As noted before, many libraries have begun to revise the furniture, setting up a desk where there are two monitors—one facing the patron on one side of the desk and the other facing the librarian on the other side of the desk. Although this is a good arrangement, it still creates a sense of separation—an alienation of the user in relationship to information and of the patron to the consulting librarian.

The reference space at Kresge Library with its single monitor and side-by-side approach minimizes physical distancing and also any feeling of inaccessibility to information sought by the patron. Second, this reference space provides more than a mere space for the patron; it affords the patron a portion of the collaborative area—whether for taking notes or working concurrently on a laptop while the librarian is also working—e.g., browsing databases together or separately. Third, the librarians at Kresge have achieved a more consultative feel, which makes reference into a process of partnering as opposed to the operating of a dispensary. This allows the patron to own the project—to be a coproducer—and to express preference for resources within a database search that appeal to the user; it allows the librarian to guide the patron, to obtain continuous feedback, and to provide better service. It ultimately emphasizes that the student is a co-worker in the process—not merely a consumer. Often, the research on reference work assumes that the practice of reference either consists of dispensing information or in providing instruction. Reference doesn't have to be an either/or situation—but rather may be practiced as a both/and process. As noted by Soo Young Rieh, "the focus of the [reference] role is moving back to user instruction in an individually-based interaction at the reference service."[16]

WHAT RELATIONAL REFERENCE IS NOT

In the recent literature, though, this "individually-based interaction" has frequently been cast in terms of the library user as customer. As such, it tends to couch the discussion within a very specific system of markets, exchange value, consumer demands, claims upon labor, and behaviors characteristically seen as historically innate to the market mechanisms of the cash-nexus. Cash-nexus means a relationship that is characterized almost entirely by monetary transactions. Thomas Carlyle, in a chapter titled "Not Laissez-Faire" in his essay on Chartism described "Cash Payment as the sole nexus between man and man."[17] When the discussion is couched in consumerist language, the dispensary model of reference is promoted and buttressed. This model is characterized by a flat mode of production by the librarian and of consumption by a consumer—with information as a mere commodity. John Budd highlights that "commodification of information has an inevitable effect. Information ceases to be seen as something that informs—something that has or conveys meaning—and, instead, is seen only as an object with an established exchange value."[18] Not only does the consumerist model promote information as a commodity but, most important, it affects the relationships between students and librarians. Budd states that "although there is a frequent rhetorical insistence on the needs of individuals, the individuals get lost in the process of identifying people as customers."[19] This process of reification (as per cultural materialistic thought by which the human is converted into an inanimate object and in which human interchange becomes that of inert forces) objectifies the user; this should not be the case. Harley and colleagues state that "academic library service should be people—rather than commodity-driven. It is all too easy to overemphasize information as a commodity at the expense of those who seek, deliver, and use information."[20]

Although relational reference has a strong service ethic, it is not "customer" service per se. Whereas relational reference emphasizes interconnectedness, the consumerist model (although possibly well intentioned) casts reference as a mode of transaction without actual relationship, which may too easily lead to objectification, to a failure to serve an individual that you do not know and in whom you are not invested, and to the dehumanization of number 0000 or of customer X. Tyckoson notes that "reference is not something that is packaged and marketed to the masses; rather, it is a service that treats every library patron as an individual with unique needs."[21]

Relational reference emphasizes the library as a community of knowledge with the individual at the center of dialogic participation, not as a marketplace of production and consumption. Thus far in the restructuring of Kresge Library, anecdotal evidence from patrons and faculty bears out the positive nature of the physical and accompanying philosophical modifications. Further evidence from a formal survey as to library quality will be available in late spring 2005. What is certain, though, is that librarians can and historically have provided quality services without the customer nomenclature.

Relational reference seeks to offer service within a human-value context removed from the "cash-nexus" mentality, minimizing the alienation of user to librarian and of each user to information. Information and labor thus become not alienated objects, and information becomes possessed knowledge within the context of a relational collaborative community.

NOTES

1. Massey-Burzio, Virginia. Reference Encounters of a Different Kind. *Journal of Academic Librarianship* 18(November) (1992): 276-280.

2. Ibid., p. 277.

3. Ibid., p. 278.

4. Ibid., p. 278.

5. Andrews, Judy C., Bowman, Michael, and Hanke, Douglas M. Around the World: Rethinking Reference: A Case Study at Portland State University's Millar Library. *Library Hi Tech News* 20(May) (2003): 13-15.

6. Bartle, Lisa R. Designing an Active Academic Reference Service Point. *Reference and User Services Quarterly* 38(Summer) (1999): 395-401.

7. Rieh, Soo Young. Changing Reference Service Environment: A Review of Perspectives from Managers, Librarians, and Users. *Journal of Academic Librarianship* 25(May) (1999): 178-186.

8. Tyckoson, David A. What Is the Best Model of Reference Service? *Library Trends* 50(Fall) (2001): 183-196.

9. Harley, Bruce, Dreger, Megan, and Knobloch, Patricia. The Postmodern Condition: Students, the Web, and Academic Library Services. *Reference Services Review* 29(1) (2001): 23-32.

10. Huwe, Terence K. Being Organic Gives Reference Librarians the Edge over Computers. *Information Today* 21(May) (2004): 39-41.

11. Wilder, Stanley. Information Literacy Makes All the Wrong Assumptions. *The Chronicle of Higher Education* 51(January 7) (2004): B13.

12. Brown, John Seely. Growing Up Digital. *Change* 32(March/April) (2000): 10-20.

13. Ibid., p. 13.

14. Harley et al., The Postmodern Condition.

15. Donham, Jean, and Green, Corey Williams. Developing a Culture of Collaboration: Librarian As Consultant. *Journal of Academic Librarianship* 30(July) (2004): 314-321.

16. Rieh, Changing Reference Service Environment, p. 184.

17. Symons, Julian, ed. *Carlyle: Selected Works, Reminiscences, and Letters.* Cambridge, MA: Harvard University Press, 1967.

18. Budd, John M. A Critique of Customer and Commodity. *College & Research Libraries* 58(July) (1997): 310-321.

19. Ibid., p. 312.

20. Harley et al., The Postmodern Condition.

21. Tyckoson, What Is the Best Model of Reference Service?, p. 190.

EXERCISES

1. Summarize this case study, stating the main points for a classmate or co-worker who knows very little about the subject. Relate this case study to your experience as a student, employee, or customer.
2. Rewrite the summary for a different audience (expert in the field, college administrator, fund-raiser) to justify implementation of relational reference in a library that has a traditional reference desk.
3. With a classmate or co-worker, role-play the case study, with one person playing the author, and the other person asking the author about his or her purpose, motivations, main points, evidence, conclusions, etc.
4. Do you agree or disagree with the main points of the case study? Do you base this on prior knowledge, opinion, author's arguments, cited evidence, intuition, or a combination of these elements?
5. Find two scholarly, authoritative sources (books or articles) that support or refute the main points of this case study. Detail the sources consulted and the search terms used.
6. Based on the evidence presented in the preceding case study, what do you think are the most significant challenges facing academic librarians involved with planning or designing service points?
7. Develop three to five interview questions that could be used to interview a practicing academic librarian about his or her experience redesigning or refurnishing a reference area.
8. Visit an academic library and observe the interactions among reference librarians and their clientele. Is the desk a barrier or a shared surface? Is the desk high or low? Is there seating for the client? Do other furnishings affect the quality of transactions?

Case Study 5

Virtual Reference: Answering Patrons' Questions Electronically

Christopher Nelson Cox

INTRODUCTION

More and more, patrons are choosing to access library materials and services from outside the library's walls. Convenience for them means logging onto a computer, searching databases by proxy, renewing materials online, and asking questions electronically. A fad for some, a necessity for others, virtual reference has blossomed and flourished in libraries, and reference librarians have had to learn and adapt.

Virtual reference is defined as "reference service delivered electronically, often in real-time, where patrons employ computers or other Internet technology to communicate with reference staff without being physically present."[1] The term *virtual reference,* also called chat and digital reference, encompasses two types of services: asynchronous, usually exemplified by e-mail reference, and synchronous or real-time virtual reference. Communication channels for real-time virtual reference include chat, videoconferencing, or voice over IP.

Virtual reference has been around since the early 1980s, but did not really catch on until 1999, perhaps as a reaction to the needs of our patrons, or to an unhealthy drop in reference statistics.[2] Not long after, librarians noted that companies were using software to respond to customers' needs in real time. Libraries saw the potential of these applications and began licensing them for their own use. Having identified a need, companies such as LSSI and even OCLC created virtual reference software and marketed it to libraries.

An Introduction to Reference Services in Academic Libraries
© 2006 by The Haworth Press, Inc. All rights reserved.
doi:10.1300/5634_05

There is no way to know how many libraries currently offer virtual reference, but the number is in the hundreds, if not the thousands. According to research independently conducted by McKiernan[3] and Francouer,[4] the number could range from 132 libraries to as many as 500. The popularity of virtual reference is evident by its popularity as a source of scholarly inquiry. A search of "library literature" reveals that, in 2004 alone, two books, five master's theses, and forty-six articles were written on the subject.

This case study does not intend to add to that load, but rather to offer an overview to those thinking of offering virtual reference, or those responsible for managing or evaluating an existing service.

NEEDS ASSESSMENT

If a library does not currently have virtual reference in place, a great deal of preparation will be required to get it off the ground. Start by considering the following: Why is it needed? Yes, libraries need to reach out to those who silently shun our physical library buildings. Yes, everyone else is doing it. However, offering virtual reference is not cheap, and it is not easy. Before bowing to peer pressure, determine the need, and whether virtual reference is the best way to fill it. Which begs the next question: Who is the target audience? Distance learning students? Students on a university campus? Conduct a survey targeted specifically at those user groups, asking them if they require an additional communication vehicle or if what is currently offered is sufficient. The few moments spent conducting a survey may save countless hours and dollars later.

The next question is probably the easiest to answer and the most prohibitive: How much is the library willing to spend? Launching a virtual reference service costs money: to pay for the committee meetings that determine the type and scope of service offered, to purchase the software, and to pay librarians to staff the service.

If it is determined that virtual reference is a necessary and affordable endeavor, the rest of the library staff needs to be on board before making any more decisions. Virtual reference is not just a reference initiative: it can affect everything from collection development to licensing.

Next, decide what level of virtual reference to be implemented. The most common option is e-mail reference. E-mail reference originally consisted of creating a reference e-mail alias and publishing it on the Web site. Librarians now use e-mail forms so questions can be easily categorized and routed. E-mail reference has been implemented at this author's previous institution, Worcester Polytechnic Institute (WPI), and current one, the University of Wisconsin—Eau Claire (UWEC) with significant success.

The lack of real-time patron interaction is a significant drawback to e-mail reference. Users' expectations of how long an answer should take may range from minutes to days. Staffing levels or question complexity may add to the response time. At UWEC, librarians staffing the reference desk check e-mail various times during their shifts. A question that arrives during regular reference hours may be answered within an hour of receipt, but late-night queries are not answered until the next morning.

Virtual reference software offers patrons and librarians alike a variety of interactive features, including chat and call alert, a notification that a patron query has arrived. Most also offer page-pushing and co-browsing capabilities, and queue management, so questions can be held until a librarian is free to answer them.[5]

The drawback, of course, is price. Virtual reference software packages are costly, not only in terms of the software and hardware required, but also in staff time and training. Prior to purchase, consult with computer networking services or the equivalent on campus. There may be issues that have not been considered, including licensing. Is the pricing determined "per seat," by the number of librarians who can simultaneously use the software, "per user," by how much customers use the service, or is it just a flat fee?[6] Who is called when there are problems? Look at reviews and consult with colleagues to determine company responsiveness. Is additional hardware necessary or will the service be hosted on a server maintained by the company? Although the latter may seem tempting, it is not recommended. System crashes fixed at the discretion of the company may result in longer downtimes and greater frustration for patrons and librarians alike.

Finally, consider the patron. Is the software easy to use? Does it require downloading of files or installation of plug-ins? Such requirements could spell doom for a virtual reference service. If at all possible, schedule a trial of the software before purchase and if possible, involve patrons in the decision-making process.

INSTANT ANSWERS@WPI

Instant messaging software serves as an inexpensive middle ground between e-mail and software-driven virtual reference. Products from companies such as AOL are free and familiar to patrons, and allow users to chat in real time. At WPI, librarians found the cost of virtual reference software to be prohibitive. Unsure of the amount of questions that would be received, WPI librarians chose AOL Instant Messenger (AIM), with the idea that if the demand was high enough, the software decision would be reconsidered at a later date. A committee of librarians met to determine staffing, policies, and name of the service. As the majority of the staff was not familiar with instant messaging programs, training and practice were required. A list of operating instructions, a Web page of policies and frequently asked questions, and an evaluation form were developed for the service.

On November 11, 2002, Instant Answers@WPI was introduced. It was announced that chat requests would be answered primarily during reference shifts. Students knew that librarians were logged in when the AIM icon on the library pages was orange. Service hours would be continued or discontinued based on its popularity and the feedback received.

WPI librarians felt justified for using free messaging software when the service received only forty-three questions through May 2003, an average of 4.5 questions per day. Problems arose due to the lack of automatic transcript logging and queuing software, but overall, the experience and responses have been positive, and the service continues today.

COLLABORATIVE EFFORTS

Participating in a collaborative virtual reference project, usually initiated by a group of libraries (consortium, state library system, etc.) is one way of offering virtual reference at a lower cost. Such collaboration also allows libraries to extend the service hours of operation, distribute staffing, and extend expertise. As of November 2003, 1,730 libraries were participating in a total of sixty-two collaborative services.[7]

Unfortunately, such collaborations are often fraught with problems. A majority of librarians have to agree both to use a particular software package and to abide by policy decisions, an act of consensus that is not always easy to achieve. Prior to the author's arrival at UWEC, librarians participated in a pilot of a statewide reference service using OCLC's QuestionPoint. QuestionPoint allows users to send e-mail messages or chat in real time. Ten university libraries throughout Wisconsin participated at a cost of $2,000 per library. For four hours each week from June through December 2002, UWEC librarians monitored QuestionPoint from their offices, separate from their normal reference hours and other duties. Only seventy-three chat sessions were recorded in that time period, an average of three questions a day. In September 2003, UWEC chose not to renew the contract on the service citing that the amount of usage did not warrant the cost. In order for future collaboration to succeed, UWEC librarians commented that staffing must be reliable; users should be alerted that they may not be addressing someone from their own institution; and staff from each institution should develop a familiarity with resources at other consortial sites.[8]

NUMBER OF QUESTIONS

As it was for Instant Answers@WPI, another concern is the number of questions a service is expected to get. In his "Global Census of Digital Reference," Janes asked libraries offering virtual reference of any kind (e-mail, chat, software-based) to report the number of questions received during three predetermined "typical" days in November 2003.[9] One hundred sixty-two services reported a total of 8,106 questions. Although this number may seem significant, the median service "answered just 16 questions over the 3-day period—-and . . . the median number of questions per day was just a little less than six."[10] Suffice it to say the volume will be low.

POLICIES AND PROCEDURES

Once the type and level of service has been determined, libraries interested in offering virtual reference need to develop policies and procedures for use of the service including users served, staffing, types of questions answered, and privacy.

The question of what users to serve should have been answered earlier. Some libraries also choose not to answer more complicated questions from people outside their institutions. When it comes to staffing there are a number of options. What will the hours of operation be? 24/7? Will extra staff need to be hired? Will librarians cover the traditional reference desk at the same time as the virtual one? What questions will be given priority: those posed in person or online? What about the types of questions answered? Will users with more in-depth questions be asked to come to the library? How will questions be referred to other departments?

Decisions concerning the privacy of patrons are the most important. Many libraries archive virtual reference sessions for training and statistical purposes. If you choose to archive, all transcripts should be treated as confidential and users should be notified that their interactions are being recorded. In fact, all policy decisions should be made clear to the patron and published on the library's Web site.

STAFF SKILLS

Running a successful virtual reference service means providing the right amount of training to staff. Two organizations have published curricula to assist reference librarians in answering questions virtually. "Rubrics for Digital Reference Service Providers," sponsored by the Digital Reference Education Initiative (DREI), were developed "to guide teaching digital reference to LIS students [and] also as a guide to training, hiring and evaluating practicing librarians and library staff with digital reference responsibilities."[11] They are presented at three levels (basic, intermediate, and advanced) and include everything from computer literacy to triage and collaboration. The Washington Statewide Virtual Reference Service Training Committee identified thirteen core competencies.[12] These included keyboard proficiency, Internet and database searching skills, multitasking, and technical troubleshooting skills.

These resources give a sense of the differences between answering a reference question electronically versus in person. The biggest difference is time. Librarians answering virtual reference questions for the first time tend to become slaves to the clock, believing that customers expect instantaneous answers. They neglect the basic tenets of the reference interview, forgetting to paraphrase and ask clarifying questions, jumping to Google rather than to equally pertinent print reference works, and worried that the patron will disappear before they have the time to answer his or her question. As Coffman and Arret note, "the average chat question still takes 10-15 minutes to answer."[13]

That said, the speed of chat may cause librarians to adjust their communication style. Using e-mail allows time to deliver a well- thought-out and grammatically correct response. In chat, one must "abandon a lifetime habit of scrupulous attention to grammar, punctuation, capitalization and spelling."[14] Since time is of the essence, responses are broken into shorter snippets. Librarians need to rephrase the question and offer frequent updates of what is being done to answer the question. The virtual patrons cannot see that the librarian is still working hard for them. To save typing time, prescripted greetings or answers to common reference questions can be developed.

Owing to the lack of face-to-face interaction, librarians have to work twice as hard to make a personal connection with the patron. Roberts believes librarians should provide their names and work on engendering empathy, since users in the virtual environment are often as frustrated as their in-person counterparts at not being able to find the information needed.[15]

STAFF TRAINING

How should training be conducted? Hirko suggests practicing chat reference with colleagues and taking "virtual" field trips to library Web sites that already offer virtual reference.[16] Logging in and asking questions of a preexisting service as a "secret patron" is also effective. Examination of archived transcripts is also useful for evaluating virtual reference encounter quality and suggesting improvements.

Librarians also need to prepare for the types of questions they will be asked. Luckily, these do not differ much from those received at traditional reference desks. Diamond and Pease analyzed e-mail reference questions received over a two-year period at California State University Chico.[17] The 450 transactions logged were divided into 11 categories. Garnering the most queries were "questions answered using standard reference resources," representing a mixed bag of general reference questions such as "Did Betsy Ross really sew the first American flag?" and "catalog lookup and use."

An analysis of 252 e-mail reference questions at UWEC submitted during a six-month period (July 1, 2003, to December 30, 2003) using Diamond and Pease's categories yielded similar results. Questions about interlibrary loans occurred most frequently (34), probably owing to the introduction of a new interlibrary loan system, followed by "catalog lookup and use" (24), and "connectivity questions" (15), the majority of which dealt with off-campus access.

MARKETING

For both new and existing services, marketing is essential. Instant Answers@WPI was announced via e-mail, posters, flyers, and an article that appeared on the front page of the student newspaper. Prominent icons to the service should be included on Web pages where students may need assistance. The results of a marketing campaign can be monitored to see if adjustments are necessary.

Assessment should be built into every aspect of virtual reference planning. Current patron feedback is needed to know whether the right decisions were made concerning level of service, software, and service effectiveness. One form of feedback is the online evaluation form. Upon completing an Instant Answers@WPI chat, patrons completed a form asking their class and location (on- or off-campus), whether they had difficulty in using the service, and their satisfaction level with the service.

SERVICE CONTINUATION

Recently, scholars have begun to question whether libraries should continue to offer virtual reference. Maxwell tells the story of an "Ask a Librarian" service which suffers from "technical glitches, low enthusiasm among librarians and even lower student use."[18] Maxwell goes on to suggest reexamination of intentions with virtual reference and "pray" for a better solution. Coffman and Arret point out that many companies have abandoned real-time customer service, and libraries are starting to follow suit. MIT, Vanderbilt, and even the Library of Congress, an early proponent of virtual reference, have reduced their service hours or pulled the plug entirely. These libraries cite the same reason that UWEC had for leaving Wisconsin's Question-Point collaborative: "the value gotten from chat services did not justify the investment."[19] Coffman and Arret believe that libraries should improve the way virtual reference is delivered, or abandon it altogether, and concentrate on improving phone reference and self-service.

No one denies that implementing virtual reference can be a costly and time-consuming undertaking. However, patrons will continue to use resources from afar. Virtual reference, at its best, is a technological tool, one of many in a reference librarian's arsenal, that reaches out to those at a distance in need of assistance.

NOTES

1. Guidelines for Implementing and Maintaining Virtual Reference Services. *Reference & User Services Quarterly* 44(Fall) (2004): 9-13.

2. Coffman, Steve and Arret, Linda. To Chat or Not to Chat: Taking Another Look at Virtual Reference, Part I. *Searcher* 12(July/August) (2004): 38-46.

3. McKiernan, Gerry. LiveRef(sm): A Registry of Real-Time Digital Reference Services. Available at http://www.public.iastate.edu/~CYBERSTACKS/LiveRef. htm. Accessed August 1, 2005.

4. Francoeur, Stephen. Index of Chat Reference Services. *The Teaching Librarian,* 2002. Available at http://www.teachinglibrarian.org/chatindex.htm. Accessed August 1, 2005.

5. Olivares, Olivia. May: Virtual Reference Systems. *Computers in Libraries* 24(May) (2004): 25-29.

6. Ibid.

7. Sloan, Bernie. Collaborative Live Reference Services. *Bernie Sloan's Digital Reference Pages,* 2004. Available at http://www.lis.uiuc.edu/~b-sloan/collab.htm. Accessed August 1, 2005.

8. Virtual Reference Survey—Reference Coordinators' Committee. Consortium of University of Wisconsin Libraries. UWEC responses. Unpublished.

9. Janes, Joseph. The Global Census of Digital Reference. *Virtual Reference Desk 2003 Online Proceedings.* Available at http://www.vrd2003.org/proceedings/. Accessed August 1, 2005.

10. McKiernan, Live Ref.

11. Digital Reference Education Initiative. DREI: Digital Reference Education Initiative. Rubrics for Digital Reference Service Providers. Available at http:// drei.syr.edu/pdf/DREICompetenciesDraft092004.pdf. Accessed August 1, 2005.

12. Washington Statewide Virtual Reference Service. Core Competencies for Virtual Reference. Available at http://vrstrain.spl.org/textdocs/vrscompetencies.pdf. Accessed August 1, 2005.

13. Coffman and Arret, To Chat or Not to Chat.

14. Hirko, Buff and Ross, Mary Bucher. *Virtual Reference Training: The Complete Guide to Providing Anytime, Anywhere Answers.* Chicago, IL: American Library Association, 2004.

15. Roberts, Brent. What Libraries Do Best: Bringing Warmth to Virtual Reference. *PNLA Quarterly* 68(Spring) (2004): 8-9, 22.

16. Hirko and Ross, *Virtual Reference Training.*

17. Diamond, Wendy and Pease, Barbara. Digital Reference: A Case Study of Question Types in an Academic Library. *Reference Services Review* 29(Spring) (2001): 210- 218.

18. Maxwell, Nancy Kalikow. The Seven Deadly Sins of Library Technology. *American Libraries* 35(September) (2004): 40-42.

19. Coffman, Steve and Arret, Linda. To Chat or Not to Chat: Taking Another Look at Virtual Reference, Part II. *Searcher* 12(September) (2004): 49-56.

EXERCISES

1. Summarize this case study, stating the main points for a classmate or co-worker who knows very little about the subject. Relate this case study to your experience as a student, employee, or customer.

2. Rewrite the summary for a different audience (expert in the field, college administrator, fund-raiser).

3. With a classmate or co-worker, role-play the case study, with one person playing the author, and the other person asking the author about his or her purpose, motivations, main points, evidence, conclusions, etc.

4. Do you agree or disagree with the main points of the case study? Do you base this on prior knowledge, opinion, author's arguments, cited evidence, intuition, or a combination of these elements?

5. Find two scholarly, authoritative sources (books or articles) that support or refute the main points of this case study. Detail the sources consulted and the search terms used.

6. Based on the evidence presented in the preceding case study, what do you think are the most significant challenges facing academic librarians considering virtual reference?

7. Develop three to five interview questions that could be used to interview a practicing academic librarian about his or her successful or unsuccessful experience providing virtual reference in an academic library.
8. Write a one-page memorandum to a hypothetical library supervisor justifying why a specific academic library should continue or discontinue virtual reference services.

Case Study 6

What They Don't Teach You in Library School: Experience Is the Real Teacher

Tammy S. Guerrero

SETTING

Purdue University Calumet is located in Hammond, Indiana, which is about thirty miles east of Chicago. This area is home to an ethnically diverse population. More than half of Purdue Calumet Students are enrolled on a part-time basis. Over 90 percent are Indiana residents. Three-fourths of Purdue Calumet students are first-generation college students. Enrollment for the spring 2005 semester was approximately 9,200 students. Purdue Calumet offers associate degrees in twenty different fields, baccalaureate degrees in 112 fields, and master's degrees in fourteen different fields of study.

The library's collection includes 257,000 volumes and over 2,500 current journal subscriptions, including electronic journals. The library is open seventy-five hours per week, including evenings and weekends. The library has a director, two assistant directors, four professional librarians, two paraprofessionals, seven full-time and three part-time clerical staff, and numerous student assistants.

Purdue Calumet librarians are held to the same standards as the classroom faculty. They publish in scholarly journals in their field and sit on and hold offices in university and library committees. They conduct research in their field and contribute to librarianship by reviewing books and presenting papers at national and international conferences. Participating in these activities enables the librarians to

An Introduction to Reference Services in Academic Libraries
© 2006 by The Haworth Press, Inc. All rights reserved.
doi:10.1300/5634_06

draw and learn from the experiences of peers, and deliver the best possible reference services to their patrons.

The library has established a reference help desk which is staffed in one-hour shifts by professional librarians, clerical staff, and a graduate assistant. There is a recently remodeled electronic classroom where instructional sessions are conducted.

OBJECTIVE

The Purdue Calumet Library offers a hands-on model of reference service designed to connect students with information needed to carry out curricular and scholarly activities. The library's objective is to develop in patrons the ability to identify, access, evaluate, and apply information. Via ongoing research and development, the library serves as the indispensable source of excellent guidance, assistance, and instruction. Many Purdue Calumet students are nontraditional students over twenty-five years of age. The library strives to reach all students and work at their level. Learning-centered policies and practices are in place, as well as continuous training for staff, including in-house training seminars, conference presentations, and poster sessions. Purdue Calumet librarians are tenured faculty members.

METHODS

The methods refer to the three steps taken by the Purdue Calumet Library to ensure that their objectives are met through strategic planning, knowledge of student demographics, and liaison work.

Strategic Planning

First, the library established a five-year strategic plan complete with a vision, a mission, and goals. The 2001-2006 vision statement is as follows:

> As the readily accessible connection between patron and information, the library will be the trusted resource for high quality information in support of the quest for academic achievement, scholarly productivity and lifelong learning.

Goals were established to answer the question, "What does the library need to achieve for our vision of quality to become a reality?" The goals support the library's vision of high-quality library services:

Goal 1: Achieve staffing ratios at or above the mean documented for peer-comprehensive institutions of higher learning and organize responsibilities to achieve optimal performance by library faculty, staff, and administrators.

Goal 2: Improve the accessibility of the library through structured outreach initiatives, including distributing information about services to the campus twenty-five times per year, arranging annual information sessions with each academic department, and hosting an annual promotional event.

Goal 3: Provide formal instruction and informal assistance in using information to 25 percent of undergraduate students and 10 percent of graduate students.

Goal 4: Enhance access to appropriate information resources supporting academic achievement, scholarship, and lifelong learning.

Goal 5: Test, integrate, and promote to faculty and students annually three new technologies or formats for providing access to scholarly information.

Goal 6: Introduce services and sponsor activities to achieve a library facility-use ratio 25 percent higher than at present for undergraduate students and 10 percent for graduate students enrolled at Purdue University Calumet.[1]

This five-year strategic plan serves as an outline, or framework for the library's services, especially reference services. The other two aspects of the threefold plan, researching student demographics and providing liaison services, were established to complete the goals established in the strategic plan.

Student Demographics

The library does research on the student body to find out about its demographic makeup, including ethnic and educational background of the family. For example, many Purdue Calumet students are first-generation college students; many work full-time and go to school either full-time or part-time. Coming to the library is not their first priority, and they do not need to waste time wandering around looking for help. Once the library has established what their library needs are, then problems may be addressed and research questions answered. Learning a bit about the background of the person being helped can make a huge difference in the reference service provided. The library then can gear its reference services to fit the needs of these particular groups.

Liaison Services

The library establishes liaisons with faculty members from all schools and departments of the university and designs its reference services to accommodate these faculty members and support their curricula. Librarians meet with their designated dean or faculty member and discuss what is being taught and what type of reference assistance, collection development, and general supportive measures the library needs to offer to benefit the students enrolled in a particular class.

The Purdue Calumet Library plans, manages, and evaluates its reference and instruction services dually. In other words, the library values instructional sessions as much as one-on-one reference interviews. The following are examples of some of the high-quality reference services offered at Purdue Calumet.

REFERENCE SERVICES

One-on-One Reference Interviews

The library offers one-on-one reference conferences with patrons on demand, or by appointment. The library also conducts instructional sessions with entire classes, or smaller groups. Humorous stories are used to help break the ice during instructional sessions. If a librarian has recently been a student, he or she can understand where students are coming from and what their concerns and fears are. This makes the instructional session very effective. Being able to relate to a student on his or her level, without "lording over" them and asking condescending questions results in effective reference transactions, and makes the reference experience more real and rewarding for the student.

Library Tours

Another effective tool is the physical library tour. When teaching an instructional session or giving face-to-face reference service, it is helpful to the student to physically walk around and see the actual library and where things are located. This makes it easier for the student to understand what he or she has just been shown in the electronic classroom, or on a public-access computer in the reference area. Although it is important to demonstrate the electronic databases, teach searching strategies, and have students perform hands-on searches, it is also helpful to have them see where things are located.

Instructional Sessions

When giving an instructional session, it is useful to show and explain various formats and styles of periodicals so the students may see for themselves, and hopefully recognize them later when seen on the library shelves. For example, a scholarly journal, weekly magazine, both in bound and unbound formats, newspapers, rolls of microfilm, and popular magazines that are displayed in vinyl binders, can be brought into the classroom, and discussed. It is also advantageous to bring in paper sources of reference materials, to stress the fact that not everything is on the Internet. At these instructional sessions, folders with Purdue Calumet Library's logo are distributed. Inside the folders are inserts and flyers with general information on them. The material in the binders is explained in detail in class, and each student is given his or her own folder to refer to at a later date. Students have commented that these folders are quite helpful. They also serve as a great marketing tool.

The best design for instructional sessions is one that fits the specific needs of the students who are coming to the session. As stated earlier, Purdue Calumet librarians are assigned as liaisons for various departments and schools within their areas of expertise. For example, one librarian may be better at technical research, so he or she teaches the instructional sessions for and serves as liaison to engineering and mathematics departments. Another librarian's expertise may be liberal arts, so that person is the liaison to that school, or specific units within that school, such as English or History. Meetings with deans, department heads, and/or faculty for the respective liaison departments gives the librarian a chance to look over their syllabi, find out what types of materials they would like the library to have in the collection, and help select material that will support and enhance their curricula. It is also vital to find out faculty research interests so that the librarians may collect for them as well.

Example of an Instructional Session

A librarian can be a liaison to another faculty member. For example, an English professor teaches a course titled, "Artists and Their Lives," a sophomore/junior-level course which details the lives of the artists Johannes Vermeer and Artemisia Gentileschi.

First, several instructional sessions can be conducted with the students, with the professor also present. Since these students are not incoming freshmen who have never used the library, they should have a general knowledge of the library's catalog and online databases. These students may have already attended a general instructional session when they were freshmen. At this point, the librarian can skip the "general" informative session, and move on to more advanced searching strategies. If students are looking for biographical information on the authors, as well as criticism and interpretation of their work, they need to be introduced to more specific databases. This is a good opportunity to hand out folders, brochures, and other marketing information, including more specific databases and advanced searching tips, such as Boolean searching. It is a good idea to include a business card so they may contact the library if they have questions.

In addition to their term papers, the students are required to read novels and/or critical or interpretive material involving the artists. An effective reference librarian would read the assigned material as well, so that he or she is well-versed in the background material. This will give the librarian an insight into what the professor has assigned. It would be wise to select books on the authors and their works to enhance the library's collections and support the curriculum.

Challenging Reference Situations

Occasionally at the reference desk, patrons present challenging situations. By using some tact and diplomacy, a reference librarian can usually diffuse these situations and derive a positive outcome from a potentially negative one. The following is a scenario that challenges a reference librarian's skills:

A reference librarian is taking her rotation at the help desk. She observes a young girl sitting at a computer workstation. The girl is very agitated. She is slamming books around, muttering obscenities to herself, and shuffling through papers in her folder.

The librarian can see that the student needs help, so she approaches her and offers assistance. The patron immediately turns to the librarian and says, "This library sucks! I can't find anything in here, and I'm going to flunk out of school now, if I don't get this paper written." The librarian sits down next to her and takes a deep breath. The student is waving her arms over her head and being very loud. The librarian attempts to calm her down by patting her arm and telling her everything will be all right. When the librarian makes the gesture to touch the patron, she recoils quickly and says, "Don't you dare touch me." The librarian draws back her hand and backs off a bit.

The librarian calmly asks the girl to explain what she needs. She shoves the syllabus at the librarian and shows her the assignment, which was given at the beginning of the semester. It is now the end of the semester, and the student has waited until the last minute to begin her research. After looking over the assignment on the syllabus, the librarian finds that the student is required to find three scholarly journal articles relating to any topic of the student's choosing about childhood psychological disorders.

The librarian logs into the computer next to the student and tells her to watch as the librarian performs a search of an online database. The librarian slowly takes her through the electronic journals and full-text databases, showing her how to search by subject and keyword. With the librarian's assistance, the student is able to readily find plenty of scholarly articles, and proceeds to print three of them. By now, not only has the student calmed down, but she is relaxing. The librarian can see the tension leaving her face, and her body language shows it as well. This person, who at first was ranting, and had recoiled at the librarian's touch was now hugging the librarian and thanking her for all her help. She told the librarian that she had "saved her life" and possibly her college career.

First, the librarian's patience and understanding helped defuse this volatile situation. She remained calm while the student was in an agitated state, and transferred this tranquility through kind words and positive gestures. The librarian did not talk down to the student, nor judge her. Most important, the librarian took the student seriously even though she was acting erratically out of frustration. The librarian took control of the situation and used both her "people" skills and the skills she learned from library school to console the patron, help her relax, and teach her how to find what she needed in a timely fashion. The student had someone to take some of her overwhelming burden and help her deal with it.

Second, the librarian used instructional skills to empower the student. She did not just find the items for the student, print them out, and send her on her merry way. She sat down with the student and taught her how to search so that she could conduct the research herself in the future. Hopefully, this miniinstructional session gave the student the confidence necessary to repeat the process for future assignments, hopefully avoiding such an emotional "ordeal."

Finally, it is clear that the librarian's attitude defused a potentially ugly situation. The librarian's empathy for this student was genuine and the student felt that right away. Once the student realized that the librarian was "feeling her pain," she regrouped and let the librarian handle the situation. The student was impressed with the fact that the librarian had the confidence that the student would be able to do it herself. The librarian entrusted the student with the knowledge that she passed along, and realized that her "tizzy" was temporary. The student appreciated the fact that the librarian saw beneath the surface and found a confident young woman. The student walked away with not only the journal articles she needed, but also with a feeling of confidence, empowerment, and satisfaction.

This same student later returned to the library and told the librarian that she had gotten an "A" on the research paper. The student has been in the library several times since then, and always stops to say hello to the librarian, and always refers to the time that the librarian helped her. This was a great ego booster for the librarian and it also scored some positive points for the library overall. This patron was frustrated, and was ready to walk out of the library, but the librarian managed to turn that attitude around to a positive experience.

Diverse Patron Groups

In addition to these specific types of situations, the library deals with a diverse group of people on a daily basis. The patrons encountered range from incoming freshmen who have no idea where anything is or how to find it, to tenured faculty members conducting extensive research. Those who fall between these extremes are undergraduates writing a paper, graduate students researching thesis topics, or general community users seeking quick answers to questions. It is important to customize library services to suit all types of patrons. The library relies on the training the librarians received in library school, and also the "people skills" gained from reference desk experience. Blending these together makes a very effective team of reference librarians.

Successful Reference Interviews

An experienced reference librarian is skilled at finding out exactly what the patron seeks. Conducting a successful reference interview is a learned skill. Patrons may ask questions that are totally unrelated to what they really want. For example, someone may approach and say, "I want to know where your books on France are." This person really wants to find out how many French soldiers were killed in World War II. Digging a little deeper by asking some general questions, a skilled reference librarian can usually find out what is really wanted. An experienced reference librarian would ask if the research is for a paper. If so, a request to see the syllabus may yield details about the assignment such as the number of sources needed to complete the paper. It is also a good idea to ask when the paper is due. This can be a deciding factor. If someone has a paper due the next day (this happens a lot), then the student is limited to what the library owns and what can be found in electronic form. If the student has started his or her research early enough, he or she can rely on interlibrary loan and document delivery services. If there is time, a librarian can take the patron's phone number and get back to him or her with information. This allows time to collaborate with fellow reference librarians, time to digest and think about what the student needs, and approach the research more logically and thoroughly.

Students can get frustrated because their professor told them they cannot use Internet sources. Because many of them have confused databases with search engines, they think they cannot use online databases. Try to explain to students that using an online database or electronic journal is not the same as using an Internet source. Conducting a successful reference interview can calm down many a nervous, frustrated patron.

In her presentation to the Reference & User Services Association (RUSA) President's Program, Catherine Sheldrick Ross summed up the reference interview as follows:

> A good reference interview is collaboration. User and librarian are equal partners in the search, with different areas of expertise. The user is the expert in the question itself and knows how the question arose, what necessary information is missing in her understanding of the topic, and how the information will be used. The staff member is the expert on the library system and the organization and retrieval of information. Both need to work together. At the end of the process, the library professional and user, by working together, have achieved a new understanding that neither could have arrived at individually.[2]

RESULTS

Reference Evaluation Cards

Through an open, warm, and friendly approach to instruction, librarians can help many students, both old and young. As part of its strategic plan, the Purdue Calumet Library constantly looks for innovative ways to provide better service. Assessing and evaluating staff and collections are ways to achieve this aim. For example, the library gathers information and statistics regarding types of reference questions asked, type of reference material used and type of patron served (faculty, undergraduate, graduate, etc). This information makes libraries aware of who they are helping, and what people need. This is a great tool for collection development. At random periods throughout the year, it is helpful to ask reference patrons to fill out evaluation cards (see Table C6.1), rating the service they have received at the reference desk.

These evaluation cards are collected, tallied, and reviewed. Feedback is given to the librarian so that he or she may get an idea of the quality of work that is being given at the reference desk. This infor-

TABLE C6.1. Reference Evaluation Cards

Reference Evaluation Question	Score
The library staff member's instruction was clear.	SA/A/U/D/SD
I am more knowledgeable now about library resources at PUC.	SA/A/U/D/SD
I was able to find an answer to my question.	SA/A/U/D/SD
I would be comfortable coming to this staff member for more help.	SA/A/U/D/SD

Key: SA = Strongly agree; A = Agree; U = Undecided; D = Disagree; SD = Strongly disagree

mation also tells that person's supervisor if there is a need to adjust a certain behavior. For Purdue Calumet librarians who are in tenure-track positions, this information is very valuable for their vitae. Tallied results keep library administration aware of what reference librarians are doing right, what areas need improvement, and which areas, if any, need to be adjusted.

Satisfaction Survey

Many libraries, both academic and public, are conducting user-satisfaction surveys. Findings from these surveys are an essential tool for assessing and improving performance. Susan Moysa states the benefits of conducting satisfaction surveys in academic libraries:

- Reference team members realize that they are evaluated by a certain set of standards.
- Reference team members recognize that assessment will be consistent and fair.
- Behavior that might have been considered adequate is now being reviewed based on the list of acceptable standards.
- With regular reviews, staff members learn to expect comparisons with previous behaviors.
- Specific examples are now possible, as are discussions about more appropriate behaviors.
- Long-term patterns of fair and poor behavior are now recognized formally.

Moysa adds that this process of evaluation will be a useful addition to the performance appraisal system and will lend itself to better customer satisfaction.[3] In the fall 2004 semester, Purdue Calumet Library conducted an online satisfaction survey for the library overall. The results were revealed to library staff, and adjustments were made to be more accommodating. Survey results are featured in Table C6.2.

CONCLUSION

Delivering quality reference service to patrons is not an easy task. Hopefully, after reading this case study, the reader will benefit from the methods used at Purdue University Calumet Library. The library established a five-year strategic plan, complete with mission statement, values, visions, and goals. A structured system provides all librarians, paraprofessionals, staff members, and students with a nononsense approach to delivering quality reference service to their patrons. The human element is a vital part of the process. It is the responsibility of reference librarians to make their patrons feel at ease, be skilled at conducting reference interviews, and offer instructional sessions to teach patrons how to access information. Finally, academic libraries must evaluate and assess their services and get feedback from those who are benefiting from the planning and managing of their libraries.

TABLE C6.2. Purdue Calumet Library Satisfaction Survey Conducted October 25-31, 2005 (585 Responses)

Survey Inquiry	Total No. of Respondents	% of Responses
1. The library staff is friendly and courteous.		
Strongly Agree	190	32
Agree	206	35
Neither Agree or Disagree	54	9
Disagree	17	3
Strongly Disagree	4	1
No Opinion	40	7

TABLE C6.2 *(continued)*

Survey Inquiry	Total No. of Respondents	% of Responses
No Response	74	13
2. The library staff is friendly and courteous.		
Strongly Agree	167	29
Agree	233	40
Neither Agree or Disagree	51	9
Disagree	6	1
Strongly Disagree	3	0.5
No Opinion	40	8.5
No Response	73	12
3. The library staff is knowledgeable.		
Strongly Agree	146	25
Agree	239	41
Neither Agree or Disagree	59	10
Disagree	17	3
Strongly Disagree	5	1
No Opinion	43	7
No Response	76	13
4. The library's collections are useful.		
Strongly Agree	149	25
Agree	224	38
Neither Agree or Disagree	58	10
Disagree	34	6
Strongly Disagree	7	1.5
No Opinion	34	6
No Response	79	13.5
5. Electronic resources provide information needed.		
Strongly Agree	140	24
Agree	236	40
Neither Agree or Disagree	67	11
Disagree	19	3

TABLE C6.2 *(continued)*

Survey Inquiry	Total No. of Respondents	% of Responses
Strongly Disagree	4	1
No Opinion	37	7
No Response	82	14
6. The interlibrary loan services meet your needs.		
Strongly Agree	97	17
Agree	142	24
Neither Agree or Disagree	86	15
Disagree	14	2
Strongly Disagree	5	1
No Opinion	156	27
No Response	85	14
7. Library equipment functions well.		
Strongly Agree	110	19
Agree	234	40
Neither Agree or Disagree	52	9
Disagree	50	9
Strongly Disagree	12	2
No Opinion	43	7
No Response	84	14
8. The Library is comfortable and pleasant.		
Strongly Agree	198	34
Agree	227	39
Neither Agree or Disagree	25	4
Disagree	25	4
Strongly Disagree	3	1
No Opinion	17	3
No Response	90	15

Note: Status of respondents: 429 undergraduate; 61 graduate; 39 faculty; 23 staff; 4 other; 29 no response.

NOTES

1. Purdue University Calumet Library Strategic Plan (2001-2006), Purdue Calumet Library Web site. Available at http://www.calumet.purdue.edu/library/. Accessed August 1, 2005.

2. Ross, Catherine S. The Reference Interview: Why it Needs to Be Used in Every (Well, Almost Every) Reference Transaction. *Reference and User Services Quarterly* 43(Fall) (2003): 37-51.

3. Moysa, Susan. Evaluation of Customer Service Behaviour at the Reference Desk in an Academic Library. *Feliciter* 50(2) (2004): 60-63.

EXERCISES

1. Summarize this case study, stating the main points for a classmate or co-worker who knows very little about the subject. Relate this case study to your experience as a student, employee, or customer.

2. Rewrite the summary for a different audience (expert in the field, college administrator, fund-raiser).

3. With a classmate or co-worker, role-play the case study, with one person playing the author, and the other person asking the author about his or her purpose, motivations, main points, evidence, conclusions, etc.

4. Do you agree or disagree with the main points of the case study? Do you base this on prior knowledge, opinion, author's arguments, cited evidence, intuition, or a combination of these elements?

5. Find two scholarly, authoritative sources (books or articles) that support or refute one of the main points of this case study. Detail the sources consulted and the search terms used.

6. Based on the evidence presented in the preceding case study, what do you think are the most significant challenges facing academic librarians involved with strategic planning?

7. Develop three to five interview questions that could be used to interview a practicing academic librarian about his or her experience administering satisfaction surveys to academic library patrons.

8. Write a one-page memorandum to a hypothetical library supervisor outlining a three-year career plan for yourself accepting a tenure-track, library faculty position.

Case Study 7

Occasional Occurrences at Owl Creek University

Debra Cox Rollins
Rusty Gaspard

INTRODUCTION

Over the past thirty years, the duties of academic reference librarians have increasingly included delivery of instruction to library users as a part of professional activity. As academic institutions give growing emphasis to the development of information-literate students, and as they struggle with identifying librarians' roles in supporting this expected student learning outcome, some libraries have shifted their focus on reference services and bibliographic instruction to more active collaboration with faculty.[1] This case study attempts to help readers think about where the divisions of reference assistance, outreach, and instruction are drawn by inviting readers to consider the following questions:

- With whom do the specific responsibilities of librarians and classroom instructors for helping students develop information literacy reside?[2]
- What specific activities that contribute to the development of information literacy occur at the reference desk?[3]
- How do librarians perform professional responsibilities for reference service, instruction, and outreach in a way that demonstrates that their library is fulfilling its role in the overall institutional mission?[4]

An Introduction to Reference Services in Academic Libraries
© 2006 by The Haworth Press, Inc. All rights reserved.
doi:10.1300/5634_07

Owl Creek University's librarians find themselves actively struggling to answer these questions.

SETTING

Owl Creek University is a fictional fifty-year-old public university located in a principally agricultural area of the southern United States. Fifteen miles from the nearest city, the university serves students commuting from within a 100-mile radius of its campus. One hundred full-time faculty teach about 3,000 students each semester. Four years ago the school began a substantive change from a two-year "feeder school" that awarded associate degrees, to an independent university offering four regular baccalaureate degrees. Additional degrees are in various stages of approval and implementation, and preparation for new upper-level courses is proceeding rapidly.

BACKGROUND

Owl Creek University Library opened forty years ago. The building, save for essential repairs, has not been renovated since its construction. As the library acquired electronic reference resources, computer workstations were installed where existing electrical outlets were located and without consideration for user convenience or comfort. The reference shelves are tightly packed, and the reference area floor space is dominated by print index volumes on special tables. The reference desk itself is tucked away around a corner and is not visible from the front door or circulation desk; students have to look for the reference librarian stationed there.[5]

The library collection itself is well-developed in support of lower-division courses and has a very high level of resources per student compared to peer institutions. The library has added online databases and a large collection of e-books to its collections and provides off-campus access to these resources. Its hours have expanded in the last academic year, but the library is still open about 25 percent fewer hours and has about half the staff of comparable institutions.[6] Twelve years ago the library established an electronic catalog; for ten years it coexisted with the card catalog. The card catalog, still dominating the center of the public services area, has not been updated in the past ten years but it is still used by students and faculty searching for materials in the library collection. The faculty and students who use the library are accustomed to meeting their information needs primarily with books and print journals.

Owl Creek librarians have faculty status and rank within the university system and serve on faculty and administrative committees. All the librarians also have assigned collection development responsibilities. The library director and cataloger take responsibility for administrative duties and seldom provide public services. The library staff also includes a paraprofessional technical assistant, a paraprofessional circulation manager, and several part-time student workers. The reference librarian's original additional duties include processing interlibrary loan requests, making book selections, and maintaining a vertical file.

Mrs. Ellen Edelson is the only reference librarian.[7] She practices a passive, conservative model of reference service.[8] The majority of library instruction occurs at the point of use. Bibliographic instruction is delivered in the form of one-shot lectures and usually only when requested by classroom professors. Once instructed in using a database, students are not encouraged to ask any follow-up questions. Mrs. Edelson does not rove the reference area and only responds to users' specific requests for assistance.[9]

Mrs. Edelson makes little effort to customize her bibliographic instruction sessions to different or to specific disciplines. Collaboration between the librarian and faculty members is rare; professors usually call Mrs. Edelson the day before or the same day that they want her to give instruction.

Despite the availability of full-text subscription databases and access to six on-line computer stations in the reference area, Mrs. Edelson always focuses on the use of print resources when demonstrating resources. When students ask for help, she usually leads them to the *Readers' Guide to Periodical Literature* and *The New York Times Index.*

Semester 1: Spring

Weeks 1-2

Mrs. Edelson offers orientation and indoctrination to students at the times posted near the library circulation desk. Approximately fifteen students take advantage of these sessions during these two weeks.

Week 4

Dr. Van Vader, who has just completed a PhD, is a new assistant professor at Owl Creek University. Dr. Vader comes into the library with twenty-five of his students. He asks Mrs. Edelson if his students can work in the library. Mrs. Edelson has no objection and concentrates on activities at her desk until students ask for help. Over the next two weeks, Dr. Vader comes to the library two or three more times with each of his sections of about twenty-five students in each group. Mrs. Gloria Goodman, volunteering in the reference department, assists students who ask for help when Mrs. Edelson is not available.

Week 8

Owl Creek's library director of fifteen years retires, and a new director, Mr. Nolan Newsome comes on board. His immediate goals are to expand library services, to make the library resources more accessible, and to make the library's public spaces more inviting and more effectively arranged.

Week 12

Mrs. Edelson begins an extended sick leave.

Week 16

Mr. Newsome is authorized to hire a new, additional reference librarian who will have specific responsibilities for instruction and coordinating outreach for information literacy.

Semester 2: Fall

Two Weeks Before Classes Begin

Mr. Walter Wright is hired to fill the new position. Since earning his graduate library degree fifteen years ago, he has worked in a college-preparatory high school. Mrs. Goodman is hired as temporary librarian to fill Mrs. Edelson's vacancy. Mrs. Goodman has worked full-time in the reference department of the public library for the past five years and is completing her last few courses for her graduate library degree. Goodman also has been an adjunct instructor of a developmental "study skills" course for conditionally admitted students at Owl Creek University for about four years, and she is familiar with the library's collection and reference services.

One Week Before Classes Begin

The print card catalog, which has been closed for at least ten years, is removed from the library.

Week 3

Mrs. Goodman is on duty at the reference desk when Dr. Vader calls to ask if he can "bring her classes" to the library today; the first session starts in about ten minutes. Mrs. Goodman has no objection to this request.

Dr. Vader and his twenty-five students arrive; most students rush to the computer workstations. The first six log onto the computers, and the others wait for them to finish. Mrs. Goodman greets Dr. Vader and asks if there are any particular materials she can help the students locate. Dr. Vader says that each student is working on an individual topic for a short paper, and he does not think they will need any special help. Dr. Vader sits at a nearby table and takes out a stack of student papers. From time to time during the forty-minute class session a student will confer with Dr. Vader about a previous assignment or test, and one or two students cautiously approach reference librarians Mr. Wright or Mrs. Goodman for help.

Over the next two months, Dr. Vader frequently brings his five classes to the library "to do research." The librarian on duty at the reference desk usually offers instruction on basic research skills or strategies to the group at large and to Dr. Vader, but each time Dr. Vader declines. Individual students begin to ask one of the librarians for help when Dr. Vader is not available, and the librarians gradually become more familiar with the details of their assignment.

The librarians are particularly concerned about the professor's direction to students to use the print edition of *Readers' Guide to Periodical Literature* to locate current magazine articles on their topics, and the professor's direction to students that they can use only one "computer resource." Owl Creek Library has access to more than fifty different electronic subscription databases but has not subscribed to any print periodical indexes, including *Readers' Guide*, for many years. Both librarians express concern to Dr. Vader that his students will be unable to meet this requirement. They offer to demonstrate the use of the electronic indexes to Dr. Vader, to whole sections of his classes, or to students individually as he might prefer. Dr. Vader responds that this is just making things easy for his students saying, "They need to rely less on those computer sources and the Internet and learn to do real research." He is insistent that there is no acceptable substitute for *Readers' Guide*.

Week 5

Dr. Elizabeth Unger has been at the university for about ten years and has recently earned her terminal degree. One morning, a flock of her students bursts (unannounced, unaccompanied, and unanticipated) into the library with an "Internet Scavenger Hunt" assignment. They wait for some of Dr. Vader's students to vacate the student workstations. Working in groups, a few ask for help logging onto the computers, and they all use the Internet browsers to go to sites such as Yahoo!, MSN, and AskJeeves. From those search engine pages, they attempt to answer specific questions such as: "How many calories should an adolescent male consume per day?" and "Who invented the sphygmomanometer?" After about twenty minutes of searching, the flock departs.

Week 8

Dr. Susan Schmidt, an associate professor in her first semester at Owl Creek University, has several years of experience working with graduate students at a major research university.[10] Mr. Wright is on duty at the reference desk when two of Dr. Schmidt's students come into the library and begin to wander among the reference books. Wright asks if he can help. The students show him a list of questions Dr. Schmidt has given as an assignment and ask how to look up the answers. Some of the questions are fairly straightforward such as "What are the library hours?" and "Does the library allow you to renew books?" Others are less so: for example, "What is ProQuest?" and, "Where can you find the *DLB*?"

Over the next two days, small groups of Dr. Schmidt's students continue to come into the library to tackle the assignment. When Mrs. Goodman assists them, she sometimes tells students what she thinks the answer should be and sometimes "Googles" for an answer that she prints out for them. When Mr. Wright works with the students he questions them closely in an effort to determine what the professor expects them to learn by answering these questions, and then tries to explain some of the answers as he leads students to particular resources. Mr. Wright disagrees with Mrs. Goodman's approach of "spoon-feeding" answers to the students, but neither librarian is certain of what kinds of answers Dr. Schmidt is looking for. Since the professor is out of town for the week and her survey course is not aimed at a specific area of the discipline, it is not possible, at the point of service, for either librarian to know the best ways to help the students. After two days of such student encounters, Wright and Goodman confer during a period of low library use.

GOODMAN: I have no idea what Dr. Schmidt expects her students to find. I don't even think they know that *DLB* stands for *Dictionary of Literary Biography*. And do I show them the print copy or how to find it through the databases? I'm afraid to do that without talking to Dr. Schmidt because you know how Dr. Vader and other teachers feel about "Internet" sources, no matter how many times we try to explain the subscription resources to them!

WRIGHT: I believe what is most important is for us to support what Dr. Schmidt expects these students to learn as a result of this activity. But the students don't seem to know and I don't have a clue either! Since we can't reach her in her office, I'm not sure how to help them with this assignment.

GOODMAN: When I was at the public library and school kids came in with an assignment like this, we'd photocopy the first assignment sheet we got our hands on, fill in the answers, and then just hand it out to the rest of the students that came later.

WRIGHT: Well, that's essentially what we're doing now, except I'm not sure how to answer some of these questions. How can you give a simple answer to a questions like "What is ProQuest?" that will make sense to students who don't understand what a periodical index is or without showing them how to use an electronic database? You can't even "Google" that question and get an answer that would make sense to them. And how can I point students to "the *Twayne* series" without explaining what literary criticism is about? And even if I do, I'm not sure this is how Dr. Schmidt would want us to approach the question. Maybe she wants them to find particular articles or books relevant to something they will study later.

GOODMAN: What should we do? If part of our job is to help students learn to use specific reference materials and apply research skills, I understand that we should try to help them at the reference desk with that underlying attitude. That's why we shouldn't just hand them a resource or tell them an answer.[11] But until we can speak to Dr. Schmidt, I think the only thing we can do is provide the most straightforward answers we can, and tell students that there is no specific answer to some of the questions. But as for helping them answer the questions that fall in between those two categories, I'm just stumped.

Week 10

Dr. Schmidt has returned from her meeting, and Mr. Wright schedules an appointment during Schmidt's office hours.[12]

WRIGHT: Dr. Schmidt, we appreciated the opportunity to work with your students while you were away, but I'm not sure we helped them find the best answers to some of the assignment questions.

SCHMIDT: I'm really sorry my students bothered you. They should have been able to find out this stuff on their own.

WRIGHT: Well, most of this group is first-year students. They may have been coming to the library for the first time. Would you be interested in having one of us do a brief orientation session for them that could give them a better foundation for answering the questions?[13]

SCHMIDT: No, I really don't have time in class for that kind of thing. They should know this before they get to college anyway.

WRIGHT: We'd like to expect that too, however, our students arrive here with wide ranges of previous library experience and some of those experiences are rather limited. If library instruction during class time won't work for you, maybe you could help me understand what you wanted the students to learn by doing this assignment. That way I'd feel more confident that we were helping them in ways that go along with your intended purposes.

SCHMIDT: Well, this was really just my way of getting the students into the library. I really didn't care about what answers they give. Again, I'm sorry they bothered you, and I won't give this assignment again.

At the end of Semester 2, the library reference area is rearranged. The reference librarian's desk is now situated in a visible, central area. Student workstations are moved into a more spacious area adjacent to the reference desk, and two more stations are added. The reference collection has been heavily weeded and print indexes deemed nonessential have been relocated for withdrawal.

Semester 3: Spring

Week 3

Dr. Vader phones the reference desk and asks if he can "bring his students to the library" for research this week. Mrs. Goodman explains that since last semester the library's use has increased to the extent that it will not be easy to accommodate multiple sessions of Vader's classes back-to-back. She suggests that one class per day would be much fairer to others using the library resources during the busiest times of the day. Dr. Vader reluctantly agrees, and over the next week his classes come in during one class period each day. Mr. Wright approaches Dr. Vader while he is in the library with his students.

WRIGHT: Good morning, Dr. Vader. I notice that you are suggesting your students use *Readers' Guide to Periodical Literature*. I just wanted to be sure you understand that our library no longer has an up-to-date subscription to this resource, and we won't be able to provide this to your students.

DR. VADER: Yes, I do; but that's the best thing for them to learn how to use. It's what they will use at the public library where many of them go to do research.

WRIGHT: I don't believe the public library still has current subscriptions to this resource, either. The public library and most libraries today use the online databases for access to periodical indexes. I'm concerned that if the students don't know how to use the periodical index databases they won't be able to satisfy your requirement to locate a periodical resource. I'll be glad to show you how this works if you have a few minutes.

DR. VADER: Maybe another time. For now, I want the students to use *Readers' Guide.* You are talking about a difference in our teaching methods and I do not want to discuss my teaching methods with you.

Dr. Vader turns his back on Mr. Wright, sits down at the reference desk, opens his briefcase, and takes out a stack of student papers.[14]

Week 4

Dr. Unger's students flock in (again unannounced, unaccompanied, and unanticipated) with an "Internet Scavenger Hunt" assignment similar to last semester's; this time Dr. Unger has provided names of specific Web sites for them to use. Most students log on to the computers and begin searching for Web sites. In some cases they reach dead links. Often the factual information the questions ask for and the information provided on the Web sites they find do not match precisely. A few students ask the librarians for help finding answers to their questions. The students appreciate the librarians' explanations for the imprecise question/answer match, but are not particularly concerned about this. They flock out again after about twenty minutes.

Week 8

Dr. Schmidt requests a one-shot instruction session on subject-related resources, especially databases, for her students who are preparing research papers. Mr. Wright provides the instruction. Dr. Schmidt expresses delight in the service, in the abundance of material available, and the ease at which it is accessed. Students are delighted to find out that information resources satisfying their professor's requirements can be accessed electronically and can be used from off campus and after library hours.

Week 18

Mrs. Edelson, who has never returned from her leave, retires after twenty-seven years of service at the library.

Semester 4: Fall

Four Weeks Before Classes

Mrs. Goodman, who has now completed her graduate library degree, is hired to fill Mrs. Edelson's vacant position.

Three Weeks Before Classes

Mr. Newsome, Mr. Wright, and Mrs. Goodman agree on a new written policy for library instruction (see Exhibit C7.1).

The two assistant librarians also concur with the director's policy that the library's first priority should be providing highest levels of service to the university's students and faculty. All library policies, old and new, are guided by the library's mission statement (see Exhibit C7.2).[15]

One Week Before Classes

The librarians offer several programs for classroom professors as part of a campus-wide in-service training day. Mrs. Goodman conducts a program explaining changes to the major database vendor—users will experience an entirely new interface this semester—and introduces several new databases that have been added to the library's resources since last year. A second program, conducted by Mr. Wright, deals with helping faculty design more effective research assignments.[16] His presentation emphasizes the value of making sure

EXHIBIT C7.1.
Owl Creek University Policy on Library Instruction

I. Library faculty provides formal instruction in the following skills required for a greater level of undergraduate information literacy:
  A. Use of the library
  B. Use of library resources
  C. Use of other available information resources
  D. Strategic approaches to research
  E. Specific skills for research and use of information resources

II. Instruction is provided in the following ways:
  A. Instructional "module" sessions on general topics
    1. These sessions are scheduled by the library at the beginning of each semester.
    2. Instructors may chose to require students to complete any or all of the modules as part of a course.
      a. This requirement should be stated in the course syllabus of the assigning instructor.
      b. Instructors should make reference librarians aware of this requirement, so that any clarification of expectations can be made early in the semester in which the course is offered.
  B. Point-of-use instruction to individual students requesting help or reinforcement in using library resources or research skills
    1. Librarians are available for assistance to students at any time the library is open for
      a. One-on-one assistance
      b. Limited telephone assistance
      c. E-mail queries
    2. When assisting individual students, librarians will refer to a copy of the instructor's assignment or syllabus in addressing specific questions regarding information resources.
      a. If the instructor does not provide the library with a copy of the assignment or syllabus, the librarian will refer to the student's copy.
      b. If a copy of the assignment is unavailable, the librarian will advise students to consult with the professor for clarification.
      c. A copy of the assignment or syllabus will be requested for future use in assisting students.
  C. Course-related library instruction (formal instruction sessions on specific resources or research skills)
    1. An instructional session is scheduled at the request of an instructor.

2. Instructors are urged to require students to attend instruction modules so that class sessions can be used to support more specific resources and skills.
3. Reference librarians will maintain a schedule of all instructional sessions.
4. Prior to the initial session, instructors need to spend thirty to sixty minutes with the librarian who will be providing the library instruction to ensure that sessions are tailored to make the most effective use of class time.
5. An assignment should accompany the session, or the session should prepare for a specific assignment.
6. These sessions need to be scheduled with as much advance notice as possible, especially when demand is greatest.
   a. The initial session should be scheduled about fifteen days in advance of the desired session so that the instructor's objectives and library services and resources can be brought together efficiently and effectively.
   b. Subsequent sessions for the same course should be scheduled seven days in advance of the desired session.
   c. The library will make every reasonable attempt to accommodate instructors.
   d. Instructors need to be present for whole-class instruction to
      i. Provide definitive answers to questions specific to content or assignment requirements
      ii. Assist the librarian with students needing redirection or individual assistance
      iii. Reinforce that the session is integral to the course
      iv. Keep abreast of what their students are learning

students have the skills needed to do research and of verifying that the library has the desired resources needed to conduct effective research *before* assignments are made. He explains the value of professors' sharing written assignments with the librarians. Finally, he offers suggestions for alternatives to the traditional research paper assignment.[17] Specifically mentioned in his presentation is research documenting the relative ineffectiveness of using "scavenger hunts" for

EXHIBIT C7.2.
Owl Creek University Library Vision
and Mission Statements

Owl Creek University Vision Statement

Owl Creek University is a public university with a focused commitment to academic excellence and development of student growth through teaching, research, and service.

Owl Creek University Mission

Owl Creek University serves its students by providing high-quality academic programs in a learning environment that fosters intellectual, professional, and personal growth as it promotes research, service, and lifelong learning.

Original Owl Creek University Library Mission Statement

Owl Creek University Library is committed to supporting students in their quest for knowledge and to enhancing the learning environment of the school.

Owl Creek University Library Services Mission
(Revised Under Leadership of Director Newsome)

Owl Creek University Library Services provides a well-organized collection of high-quality resources, professional staff, instruction, and other services to support a learning environment in which instruction and research can excel. In its selection of resources and services, Owl Creek University Library Services seeks collaboration with the faculty, both as individual instructors and as various faculty departments, committees, and other academic units.

developing students' research skills.[18] A schedule of voluntary orientation and general instruction sessions for the upcoming semester is handed out along with the librarians' contact information for faculty who would like to plan more specific course-related instruction sessions.

Week 4

Dr. Vader phones the reference desk and speaks to Mr. Wright. He asks if he can bring his classes to the library as he did last semester. Since the library's general orientation sessions instruct students in use of the library's online catalog and a general database, Mr. Wright suggests that Dr. Vader's students could benefit from one of these sessions, but Dr. Vader says his students are requesting class time just to use the library. Mr. Wright asks if, during the first session for each group, he can take time to give students some general ideas about useful resources and research methods. Dr. Vader agrees, but says that he still wants students to avoid using "computer sources." The various sections of Dr. Vader's classes are scheduled at staggered times over the next week. Dr. Vader's written assignment still directs students to *Readers' Guide* and specifies that their resource material contain no more than one "computer source."

Weeks 5 and 6

Library director Newsome, accompanied by one of two librarians, gives presentations at several department faculty meetings. The presentation includes basics of using subscription databases to locate full-text journal articles. Some faculty begin to express a growing understanding of the different types of online resources and a new awareness that journal article content is the same for both actual print articles and full-text articles retrieved from databases.

Week 9

Some of Dr. Schmidt's students ask for help locating resources for their research papers. The papers are due in two weeks.

Last Week of Classes

Mr. Wright distributes the upcoming semester's schedule for voluntary orientation sessions and invites faculty to plan course-related instruction.

Semester 5: Spring

One Week Before Classes Begin

Library director Newsome and one of the other librarians make presentations at remaining department faculty meetings. The schedule for orientation sessions is distributed and the invitation for collaboration is made at each meeting. Over the next two weeks, many faculty members call or come by the library to request course-related instruction and schedule time for planning with one of the two librarians.

The schedule for course-related instruction sessions starts to fill immediately and seeing this, Mrs. Goodman and Mr. Wright agree that during peak library-use hours at least one librarian needs to be available for reference assistance and only one of them at a time should do instruction. They further agree that unless there is an extreme and extenuating need, they will each be responsible for no more than two instruction sessions per day to allow adequate time for planning and preparation for each different session and time to perform their other duties.

Week 4

Mr. Wright is on duty at the reference desk when Dr. Vader calls to see if he can bring his classes to the library. There are only a few times available on the schedule that match the times his classes meet.

WRIGHT: Dr. Vader, would you consider letting us provide some instruction to your students during those time periods? That would give them some ideas about where to find materials on their topics and demonstrate some skills they need for searching for them. Then they might feel more confident about coming to the library to do research independently.

DR. VADER: Well, if that is the only way you'll let me bring them, I guess so.

Dr. Vader's students are scheduled into the library during the fifth and sixth weeks of classes.

Week 5

Dr. Vader and his students do not show up at any of the previously scheduled times.

Week 6

Dr. Unger's new students flock in with the same "scavenger hunt" assignment from last semester. Dr. Vader and his students again do not arrive for their scheduled sessions. Phone calls to his office and e-mail messages are not answered. At the end of the week Dr. Vader calls the reference desk and speaks to Mrs. Goodman.

DR. VADER: I'm sorry I was not able to bring my classes on the days I had scheduled. May I bring them in this week?

GOODMAN: Dr. Vader, we really don't have space in the library for whole sections of your classes this week. I'm sorry you had to miss the original dates. Would you like to reschedule?

DR. VADER: Well they really don't need any special instruction or help, just time to do research. They keep telling me they can't get to the library if I don't let them do research during class time.

Mrs. Goodman reschedules Dr. Vader's class sections for the available times during Week 7.

Week 7

Dr. Vader and his students arrive at some of the scheduled times; however, no instruction is provided because the librarians have already overscheduled their availability this week. Students still ask for help using *Readers' Guide* and for help locating books and periodical articles for their various research topics.

Mr. Wright and Mrs. Goodman explore ways to deal with this ongoing situation.[19] They verify that the two libraries nearest Owl Creek University no longer maintain print subscriptions to *Readers' Guide*. Since Mrs. Goodman has had the most satisfactory communication with Dr. Vader in the past, it's agreed she'll try to reach out to him one more time. In a scheduled appointment at Dr. Vader's office, Goodman explains the necessity of advance scheduling and the ways she believes Vader's students could benefit from librarian instruction. She also explains, again, the relative uselessness of referring students to *Readers' Guide*. Goodman reports to Wright that the meeting ended cordially, but that nothing was said to indicate that Dr. Vader will change his directions to students. The two librarians agree that any further attempts to work with this professor should be initiated by Vader himself and that efforts to accommodate his requests will be made within the guidelines of the library's instruction policy.

Week 10

Some of Dr. Schmidt's students come in individually and ask the librarian at the reference desk for help locating material for their research papers. A few of them indicate that they know the kinds of resources they are expected to find (books and journal articles) but have no idea about how to locate them in the library collection. Their research papers are due in two weeks.

Week 12

Mr. Wright sends a schedule of voluntary library sessions for the upcoming semester to all faculty and invites planning for course-related instruction. Wright also advertises a newly designed electronic tutorial that covers some of the basic concepts and skills that students need for all research assignments.

Semester 6: Fall

One Week Before Classes

Library director Newsome, Mrs. Goodman, and Mr. Wright present an orientation program on library services and resources to Owl Creek University's new faculty. All faculty receive the schedule for the new semester's voluntary orientation sessions and are invited to collaborate on plans for course-related instruction. The new library tutorial is also advertised.

Weeks 1-2

Professors begin calling to schedule course-related instruction sessions. When they call, the librarians discuss new instruction opportunities. Starting with this semester, two courseware-delivered tutorials are offered as a supplement to the orientation session. Librarians explain they believe that students who take advantage of these tutorials will be better prepared for subsequent instruction for skills and resources related to specific course assignments. Some faculty members try this new approach. Others request the librarians deliver the content of the orientation session to the entire class during a course session. The librarians are willing to accommodate most requests, as long as adequate preparation time is allowed for course-related instruction, and as long as the reference desk is staffed during the times of peak library use.

Week 4

Dr. Vader calls and asks if he can bring his classes to the library for instruction. Mr. Wright takes the call and schedules the classes according to the professor's preferences. No more than two of Dr. Vader's classes are scheduled on the same day.

Week 5

Dr. Vader and his students arrive at some of the times scheduled. Mr. Wright walks students through the process of topic selection and demonstrates several helpful resources. He also demonstrates one general periodical index database and how to retrieve a full-text article. The actual article in a print periodical is compared to the document retrieved from the database. After students begin to work individually, Dr. Vader approaches Mr. Wright.

DR. VADER: I see how using the computer material could benefit my students. I still don't want them to rely too heavily on the computer for information, though. They need to know how to use books, too.

WRIGHT: I understand that expectation. We would not want students to rely just on information from Web sites, either. But the periodical database I showed them only reproduces the articles that are in journals originally. This really is not just a computer source or Internet site; it is just a new way to find journal articles. When you have more time, I'd like to show you another resource that I think your students will find very helpful for choosing and researching topics for your assignments.

Week 6

Mr. Wright and Mrs. Goodman are both on duty at the reference desk during a high-use period when Dr. Schmidt's students, in groups of two and three, come in with an assignment to find one of three specific journal or newspaper articles. They have been told that this assignment must be completed and turned in within two hours. Some students go directly to the computer workstations, log-in, and use various search engines to try to locate the articles with no success. Eventually, each group approaches the librarians for help.

Both librarians work together to help students. In the case of the first item, the librarians seem to locate the right article but there is a difference in some spellings. Two other articles are apparently located, but the dates listed in the citations given by Schmidt are different from the dates on the articles identified. Only one article can be retrieved as a full-text document through the library's subscription databases. Another can be located only by using an advanced search technique in a seldom-used database. Dr. Schmidt is phoned in her office; the librarians explain the discrepancies and the assignment is clarified.

DR. SCHMIDT: Thanks for helping students figure this out. I appreciate your support!

WRIGHT: You're welcome. We just want to be sure the students are finding what you wanted. Would you like one of us to come to your class to show them how to do this kind of searching in the future?

DR. SCHMIDT: No, but thanks, anyway. I think they can figure this out on their own, and if not, I know they can count on you all for help when they need some.

By the end of Semester 6, collected statistics show that both numbers of reference queries and numbers of students receiving instruction from the librarians have doubled since Semester 1. The library's gate count and database access reports show a corresponding increase. Mr. Wright and Mrs. Goodman are often stretched to their personal limits regarding the number of faculty and additional library responsibilities they are expected to assume while continuing to give priority to reference and instruction activities. Although Mr. Newsome is appreciative and supportive of these two librarians' efforts, he reports that budget restraints will not allow him to consider hiring another librarian for at least one more academic year. As a means of making more effective use of the materials budget, the director also announces that he has decided to subscribe to a less expensive set of databases (with a very different user interface) next semester.

CONCLUSION

Mr. Wright, Mrs. Goodman, and Mr. Newsome agree that the reference librarians' greatest ongoing challenge will be to correctly anticipate and prepare to meet the changing demands of the classroom faculty and their assignments. They know that at least three professors will continue to demonstrate different expectations for library service.

The Owl Creek University librarians therefore decide their best course of action to address this challenge is to continue to follow their instructional policy and offer reference services that are aligned with this policy as closely as possible. They agree that ideally, classroom faculty expecting students to use resources beyond the class texts should recognize the limits of their students' abilities for doing what each defines as acceptable research and share the responsibility for helping students develop these abilities. They also agree that there will be a continuing need to educate the classroom faculty about changes in the way information is stored, organized, retrieved, and delivered.

The librarians agree that they have responsibility for maintaining cordial and professional relationships with the classroom faculty that will encourage faculty to share their assignments and learning objectives with the librarians. They agree that as often as possible their reference services should be provided in a way that supports the intentions of classroom faculty. Finally, the librarians agree that, within the limits of their available resources, their activities do support the library's mission and its contribution to the mission of Owl Creek University.

NOTES

1. Bell, Steven and Shank, John. The Blended Librarian: A Blueprint for Redefining the Teaching and Learning Role of Academic Librarians. *College & Research Libraries News* 65(July/August) (2004): 372-375.

2. Association of College & Research Libraries. Objectives for Information Literacy Instruction: A Model Statement for Academic Libraries. 2001. Available at http://www.ala.org/ala/acrl/acrlstandards/objectivesinformation.htm. Accessed August 1, 2005.

3. Johnson, Kristin and Fountain, Kathleen Carlisle. Laying a Foundation for Comparing Departmental Structures Between Reference and Instructional Services: Analysis of a Nationwide Survey. *College & Research Libraries* 63(3) (2002): 275-287.

4. Katz, William A. *Introduction to Reference Work*. New York: McGraw-Hill, 1997, pp. 12-13.

5. Reference and User Services Association. Guidelines for Behavioral Performance of Reference and Information Service Providers. 2004. Available at http://www.ala.org/ala/rusa/rusaprotools/referenceguide/guidelinesbehavioral.htm. Accessed August 1, 2005.

6. National Center for Education Statistics. IPEDS Executive Peer Tool and Peer Analysis System. Available at http://nces.ed.gov/ipedspas/. Accessed August 1, 2005.

7. Benson, Larry and Butler, H. Julene. Reference Philosophy vs. Service Reality. In William A. Katz and Ruth A. Fraley (Eds.), *Conflicts in Reference Services* (pp. 83-92). Binghamton, NY: The Haworth Press, 1985.

8. Neway, Julie. *Information Specialist As Team Player in the Research Process*. Westport, CT: Greenwood Press, 1985, p. 12.

9. Reference and User Services Association. Professional Competencies for Reference and User Services Librarians. 2003. Available at http://www.ala.org/ala/rusa/rusaprotools/referenceguide/professional.htm. Accessed August 1, 2005.

10. Association of College & Research Libraries. The Mission of a University Undergraduate Library: Model Statement. 1987. Available at http://www.ala.org/ala/acrl/acrlstandards/missionuniversity.htm. Accessed August 1, 2005.

11. Elmborg, James K. Teaching at the Reference Desk. *Portal: Libraries and the Academy* 2(July) (2002): 455-464.

12. Isaacson, David. Conflicts Between Reference Librarians and Faculty Concerning BI. In William A. Katz and Ruth A. Fraley (Eds.), *Conflicts in Reference Services* (pp. 117-128). Binghamton, NY: The Haworth Press, 1985.

13. Baxter, Pam M. The Benefits of In-Class Bibliographic Instruction. *Teaching of Psychology* 13(February) (1986): 40-41.

14. Johnson, Eric. Promoting a Positive Image: Hints for the New Reference Librarian in Dealing with Faculty. In William A. Katz and Ruth A. Fraley (Eds.), *Conflicts in Reference Services* (pp. 135-141). Binghamton, NY: The Haworth Press, 1985.

15. Association of College & Research Libraries. Standards for Libraries in Higher Education. 2004. Available at http://www.ala.org/ala/acrl/acrlstandards/ standardslibraries.htm. Accessed August 1, 2005.

16. LOEX Clearinghouse for Library Instruction. Instruction Links. Available at http://www.emich.edu/public/loex/islinks/islinks.htm. Accessed August 1, 2005.

17. Klopfer, Lisa. Effective Assignments Using the Library or, You Don't Get Muscles from a Tour of the Gym. 2002. Available at http://people.emich.edu/ lklopfer/ assignments.html. Accessed August 1, 2005.

18. Carlson, D. and Miller, R.H. Librarians and Teaching Faculty: Partners in Bibliographic Instruction. *College & Research Libraries* 45(November) (1984): 483-491.

19. Leonicio, Maggie. Going the Extra Mile: Customer Service with a Smile. In Celia Hales Mabry (Ed.), *Doing the Work of Reference: Practical Tips for Excelling as a Reference Librarian* (pp. 51-63). Binghamton, NY: The Haworth Press, 2001.

EXERCISES

1. Summarize this case study, stating the main points for a classmate or co-worker who knows very little about the subject. Relate this case study to your experience as a student, employee, or customer.
2. Rewrite the summary for a different audience (expert in the field, college administrator, fund-raiser).
3. With a classmate or co-worker, role-play the case study, with one person playing the author, and the other person asking the author about his or her purpose, motivations, main points, evidence, conclusions, etc.
4. Do you agree or disagree with the main points of the case study? Do you base this on prior knowledge, opinion, authors' arguments, cited evidence, intuition, or a combination of these elements? Does your personal style identify with or resemble Mrs. Edelson, Mr. Wright, or Mrs. Goodman?
5. Find two scholarly, authoritative sources (books or articles) that support or refute the main points of this case study. Detail the sources consulted and the search terms used.
6. Based on the evidence presented in the preceding case study, what do you think are the most significant challenges facing academic librarians collaborating with teaching faculty?
7. Develop three to five interview questions that could be used to interview a practicing academic librarian about his or her expe-

rience working with teaching faculty and/or integrating library instruction into a college curriculum.

8. Write a one-page memorandum to new and existing teaching faculty outlining instructional and reference consultation services available through a hypothetical academic library.

Case Study 8

Uninvited Change:
The Governors State University
Library's Evolving Reference
and Technology Desk

Paul Blobaum

INTRODUCTION

Governors State University is an upper-division university with master's and bachelor's programs, located in the south suburbs of Chicago. Founded in 1969, Governors State University's mission is to make higher education accessible to working adults, and to serve those who are underserved by higher education. Students commute to the nonresidential campus for late afternoon, evening, and weekend classes. The average student among 6,000 undergraduate and graduate students is a thirty-five-year-old working mother. Students arrive with various levels of competency with technology, ranging from those who have very limited experience with using computers, to those who are very competent.

The university library serves the student body and nearly 200 full-time faculty. Librarians have tenure-track faculty appointments with an assignment of duties. A university-wide strategic plan was implemented in 2001 with an initiative to develop online degree programs and to move more fully into Web-enhanced courses as well as online courses across all academic programs. Subsequently, the library dean's role was expanded to include additional responsibilities for carrying out technological initiatives, which included grant writing to secure

An Introduction to Reference Services in Academic Libraries
© 2006 by The Haworth Press, Inc. All rights reserved.
doi:10.1300/5634_08

funds to implement seventeen new "smart" and "genius" classrooms on campus, new computers for the library, the appointment of a new Information Technology Policy and Planning Committee (ITPPC), in addition to the standard library responsibilities. At Governors State, new technologies and programs were particularly challenging in a period of appropriation cuts of over 28 percent in three years by the state legislature.

State Funding

During the years 2002 to 2004, Illinois cut spending for public higher education by 18 percent statewide. In addition to cuts during this time, the state also implemented rescissions where appropriated funds were asked to be returned to the state to fill budget shortfalls toward the end of the fiscal year. Planning and budgeting for effective library services during this time was challenging for university and library administrators. During the academic year 2000-2001, the library staff consisted of thirty-eight full-time employees, which included nine faculty librarians and twenty-nine civil service employees. In the ensuing three-year period, the library's materials and personnel budget was reduced by 26 percent over 2000 levels, resulting in a staff reduction to thirty-one full-time equivalents (FTE), including six library faculty positions. This workforce reduction was accomplished mostly through attritions and retirements.

OBJECTIVE

The objective for the reference department was to respond to the strategic goals of the university when planning and implementing its own strategic initiatives and programs. The reference department's goal was to focus on the technology and knowledge-based resource needs of its clients. Reaching this goal and objective required the reexamination of time-tested traditional library services, long-standing staffing levels, competencies of personnel, and experimentation with innovative services not usually associated with an academic library's reference service.

Furthermore, the main objective was to maintain the same level of high-quality reference service during all hours of library operation. The reference desk is staffed seventy-five hours per week, during all hours the library is open. As staffing levels in the library changed due to retirements and attrition, there was some discussion as to whether the reference desk needed to be staffed with trained personnel during all hours of library operation. A key issue was how to maximize the time of reference librarians when their numbers were reduced from nine with a reference assignment to five.

METHODS

It is difficult to present a clear-cut case history of how reference services were transformed from point A in 2000 to point B in 2004. During this time, multiple environmental factors and strategic focuses shaped reference service in the university library. However, two significant turning points affected planning for library reference services.

Technology Support Partnership

The first major turning point occurred in fall 2001 when the university library partnered with the College of Education to provide technology support to education students in order to meet technology standards set forth by the National Council for Accreditation of Teacher Education (NCATE). Up until this time, the reference desk had been staffed by faculty librarians and three full-time library technical assistant III (LTA-III) positions. The LTA-IIIs provided direct reference service as well as supported the library faculty in special projects such as selecting materials, preparing purchase requests, weeding, and inserting periodic updates in loose-leaf reference materials.

By partnering with the College of Education, the university library was able to expand its publicly accessible Internet-connected workstations to thirty-seven; implement access to Microsoft Office applications; and acquire scanners. Computer workstations and microfilm/microfiche readers scattered throughout the library were relocated to one central location surrounding the reference/technology service areas.

To support the added technology and increased need to support students in using technology, the reference desk was reorganized into two service areas: the technology desk and the reference desk. Reference LTAs were reassigned primary responsibilities for technology support, and additional LTAs from acquisitions/serials and cataloging departments were reassigned some responsibilities at the technology desk. Reference librarians were assigned primary responsibility for answering reference inquiries; technology desk staff were assigned responsibility for troubleshooting computers, printers, copy machines, coin changers, and other machinery, as well as supporting the use of Microsoft Office software. A plan was devised to offer short technology workshops for students on Word, PowerPoint, Outlook, and other products to support learning and classroom project needs.

About the same time that the reference desk was reorganized to support additional technology for students, the university cut the position of the technology trainer who previously taught Microsoft Office software classes to university faculty and staff. The administration turned to the library for support in this area. The library expanded the technology trainer's targeted audiences from staff-only to the training needs of faculty, staff, and especially, students.

Librarians and LTAs volunteered to learn particular products and offer workshops according to their areas of interest and expertise. A reference librarian was designated as the coordinator of the workshops. The librarian who was responsible for coordinating reference assumed responsibility for the newly created reference/technology service desk. New job descriptions were written and approved by the Human Resources Department, and library staff transitioned to new roles and responsibilities.

LTA staff at the newly devised technology desk received online training on Microsoft Office and Web development products. Staff were cross-trained on common computer troubleshooting problems, and a system was devised to document and refer equipment problems to the university's print shop staff, who manage service contracts for microfilm, photocopy, and change machine equipment.

Virtual Reference Services

In order to meet the needs of distance-learning students during this time, reference librarians experimented with virtual reference services. During the 2001-2002 academic year, virtual reference was implemented using the Human Click platform and utilizing reference desk staff during scheduled desk times. Due to assorted problems with the software and the reduction in coverage of the reference desk from two reference staff to one at a time, this service was not continued. In the 2003-2004 academic year, the virtual reference experiment was reinstated by collaborating with MyWebLibrarian, an Illinois-based multitype library consortium that provided virtual reference services. Volunteer librarians and LTAs staffed the service, mostly off desk, for seven hours per week; other libraries in the consortium covered the remaining hours, six days per week. This collaboration met with some success, but due to very low documented usage by Governors State University students toward the end of the consortium's contract year in spring 2004, participation was discontinued for the 2004-2005 academic year. A contributing factor was that other participating academic libraries pulled out of MyWebLibrarian due to the same financial constraints experienced by Governors State University.

Online Learning Paradigm Shift

The second turning point in the evolution of the reference/technology desk was the university's strategic initiative for online learning. WebCT was implemented as the online learning platform in 1999, the same year the library introduced off-campus access to online library subscription databases. By 2001, university faculty, deans, and administrators realized the university was falling further and further behind regional and national competitors in online learning. More resources were needed to make the leap to online degrees and to support them with ancillary services. An innovative proposal was implemented in 2002 to assess a $10 strategic initiative fee per credit hour which raised $900,000 in new funds in the first year. The Center for Online Teaching and Learning (COTL) was created with one administrative coordinator and two instructional development coordinators. These positions provided training and curriculum development support for faculty and students using WebCT. Initially, little collaboration occurred between the online learning implementation and the university library, except that the library used the WebCT platform to promote its E-Reserves service, and had increasingly been asked to troubleshoot problems accessing online course components. COTL developed asynchronous online troubleshooting help and tutorials, but reference staff gave real-time assistance by phone.

A reference librarian was recently designated as the coordinator of the virtual conferencing platform Elluminate Live! and plans are under development to provide reference desk support for this software.

To address the objective of staffing the reference/technology desk at all times the library was open, it was decided to utilize LTA staff to open the library in the morning, and staff the desk until 11 a.m. with single coverage. Statistics had indicated that the hours of 11 a.m. to 1 p.m. showed increased activity. Reference librarians or LTAs were scheduled to staff the desk from 11 a.m. to 8 p.m., with double coverage of a reference librarian and an LTA, or two LTAs. LTAs would staff the library from 8 p.m. to closing.

LTAs from the technical services area would be utilized to open the library and expected to be competent in locating materials in the online catalog, troubleshooting photocopy machines and network printers, and giving basic instruction on how to find articles and locate materials using the library's online databases and catalog. As additional reference/technology desk staff were hired to replace those who had left, the role of technical services LTAs would be reduced; but they would be called upon when needed to fill in during staff meetings and illnesses. In order to provide a knowledge base to support the reference/technology desk, a three-ring reference notebook was developed with information on answering questions on using WebCT, searching online databases, identifying student and staff's library barcode number, logging on to library databases from off campus, and handling problem patrons. A "librarian on call" was designated as the first "go-to" librarian for reference backup. The on-call librarian needed to be available somewhere in the library from 9 a.m. until closing or until another librarian came on duty at the reference desk.

RESULTS

The initial result of changes to the reference desk was mixed. Questions arose as to whether the LTA-IIIs who previously had done reference work would be able to continue to do reference work; or would they only answer technology questions and teach workshops. A sensitive issue was the level of responsibility the newly assigned

LTA-I and LTA-II positions could assume under the civil service classification, which are statewide standards. Could they answer reference questions and help library patrons doing literature searches? Could the LTA-Is and LTA-IIs open the library and staff the reference/technology desk by themselves? Librarians ruminated over the perceived loss of LTA-III support in selection and special projects, and how end users would confuse faculty-rank librarians with civil service staff. Initially, conceptual lines were drawn to separate librarian level service with civil service level service which caused some conflict.

Initially, the two library computer technical support persons were included in the assignment to the technology desk and reporting to the reference librarian. However, this soon proved unworkable as their efforts were needed in focusing exclusively on managing the library's information infrastructure.

Slowly, over time, the initial reservations and roadblocks have been worked through by continually focusing on library users instead of changes in the library work environment. It soon became clear that library users do not pay attention to signs that designate one side of the reference desk as "technology desk" and the other as "reference desk." To the library user, it doesn't matter if you are a librarian or a LTA-I sitting behind the desk; they need help with the reference or technology need at hand. The reference/technology desk staff's approach has evolved to what can be described as a team approach: reference and technology questions are addressed by the staff person at the desk who was directly asked the question; questions are referred on to the appropriate librarian or technology staff person who has more expertise in the area, when needed.

The technology workshops have also had mixed results. Since the workshops were offered for free, people who registered for them tended to not show up. Library workshops have consistently had very low attendance, with occasional exceptions. What has seemed to work well is that reference/technology staff makes themselves available for one-on-one tutorials on an as-needed basis. Another model is bringing workshop-type training sessions into the classroom. A typical example can be found in College of Education coursework when the whole class needs to acquire a new technology skill in order to complete assignments.

The concerns of librarians over the loss of help with doing selection, collection development, and updating reference loose-leaf materials eventually dissipated, ironically also because of budget constraints: Loose-leaf reference materials have been canceled in favor of online access. Because of budget cuts, there were little funds available for materials selection, so most materials selection focused on the requests of teaching faculty and updating older editions of books already in the collection. Reference librarians have developed workshops of one to two hours on various topics such as Microsoft software products, APA citation style, and plagiarism.

The utilization of library reference/technology desk staff for frontline help desk support for WebCT has been very successful overall, and continues to evolve. Reference desk staff noticed a reduction in fielding questions about accessing WebCT following the implementation of online tutorials and help screens. For those who never set foot on campus, the option of calling the reference desk during the hours of library operation has been very helpful. The library recently acquired access to the software which the Information Technology Services Department uses in creating a "help desk ticket" for documenting and tracking problems with hardware, software, and off-campus access. These issues are beyond the expertise of reference desk staff. The software should provide a move effective continuum of support for resolving technical issues.

It is difficult to measure the results of the evolution of the reference desk quantitatively. Reference statistics and entrance gate counts do not measure the effects of reference service changes, except to keep the user satisfaction high. In 2004, the library conducted a user-satisfaction survey of faculty, staff, students, and community users. Responses were solicited through blind surveys and focus groups. The library's reference service was rated very highly among all users in both qualitative and quantitative data.

One measure of success is the popularity of the library's computer area of thirty-seven workstations. Students often prefer to use the library rather than the academic computing services lab next door because they have received help in using Microsoft Office products, and help in working on technology projects from reference desk staff. At peak times there is a waiting line to get one of the computers, and so the addition of more computers is likely in the near future.

The impact on the morale and work of the reference desk staff is also difficult to measure. No formal satisfaction survey has been conducted among library staff. Some technical service LTAs saw the opportunity to work on the new technology desk as an advancement of their career, and the opportunity to expand their skills. Others were not as enthusiastic or comfortable in working in a public-service area, especially about being asked reference questions. The designation of a "librarian on call" during trimester interim periods and when needed helped to ensure support was available to all staff when needed. Implementing more and more technology can be interesting, fun, and challenging. It can also be very frustrating when equipment malfunctions, networks go down, and when workshops are not as well attended as one would hope.

In fall 2004, a new partnership between the library and the writing center involved writing a grant to provide drop-in consultations with writing-center tutors in the library. Although grant support was not forthcoming, drop-in writing consultations were nevertheless implemented a few weeks into the fall 2004 trimester. The writing center tutors are available in a separate consultation area during scheduled times, and reference staff and writing center staff refer students to each area, as needed. An innovative online writing consultation service and virtual reference service using Elluminate Live! is being planned.

CONCLUSION

Overall, the library has established a leadership role in all areas of academic computing services. Building on the success of technology initiatives, the library dean was asked by the provost to assume leadership for academic technology on campus, and implemented and currently chairs the Information Technology Policy and Planning Committee (ITPPC). The library dean has written several grants to support academic computing services, resulting in the implementation of seventeen "smart" and "genius" classrooms on campus. Reference/technology desk staff provide orientation and training on the use of classroom podium technology. Other reference librarians serve on key subcommittees of the ITPPC, as well as other university committees and the Faculty Senate.

During this era of great financial pressures and competition in public higher education, the library reference desk plays a crucial role in advancing technological and knowledge-based competencies for faculty, staff, and students and in supporting their success at Governors State University. Reference services staff are challenged by continual training on new systems and constant monitoring of developments on the horizon. Attendance at professional conferences such as EDU-CAUSE, meetings of local and regional library associations, and other educational opportunities such as online learning have turned out to be good investments of time and resources by the university library. Continuing education is crucial to retooling reference desk staff, resulting in innovative ideas, new energy, and refocused priorities as the library prepares for invited and uninvited future changes in reference service.

EXERCISES

1. Summarize this case study, stating the main points for a classmate or co-worker who knows very little about the subject or who has not read the case study. Relate this case study to your experience as a student, employee, or customer.

2. Rewrite the summary for a different audience (expert in the field, college administrator, fund-raiser).

3. With a classmate or co-worker, role-play the case study, with one person playing the author, and the other person asking the author about his or her purpose, motivations, main points, evidence, conclusions, etc.

4. Do you agree or disagree with the main points of the case study? Do you base this on prior knowledge, opinion, author's arguments, cited evidence, intuition, or a combination of these elements?

5. Find two scholarly, authoritative sources (books or articles) that support or refute the main points of this case study. Detail the sources consulted and the search terms used.

6. Based on the evidence presented in the preceding case study, what do you think are the most significant challenges facing academic librarians involved with online learning?

7. Develop three to five interview questions that could be used to interview a practicing academic librarian about his or her experience providing reference and instructional assistance to online learners.
8. Write a one-page philosophy statement for providing reference and instructional services to online learners.

Case Study 9

Common Queries

Marilyn Schoot-Castle

For training purposes, since 1998 the Fraught Library has collected sample queries from students and faculty. These samples are
used to prepare new reference librarians for the tasks ahead. For the
sake of scholarship, we offer the examples that follow, along with
commentary from myself and other experienced staff. These queries
came to the library via e-mail, by phone, and from walk-in customers.

WALK-INS VERSUS E-MAILED QUERIES

Certain questions, quite common from walk-in customers, are surprising via e-mail. For example, new reference librarians on desk
duty may hear, "Where is the bathroom?" often enough in the first
week to answer automatically. But the first time that question comes
via e-mail, the novice is confused and seeks help. Experienced professionals know that "down the hall and to the left" will be correct for
57 percent of such queries, and we cannot reasonably expect a higher
success rate under the circumstances (see Figure C9.1).

E-mail questions follow certain patterns and one can guess the
facts about customers based on their queries. What can you discern
from the following? "I need an article comparing Faulkner's *Absalom, Absalom!* to Hemingway's *The Sun Also Rises,* and it should be a
pretty obscure article. I need it before Friday. Can you help?" Clearly,
the supplicant is an undergraduate (in this example, a young male),
up against a deadline, and perfectly willing to plagiarize an entire paper. He is an English-lit major but probably by default. He is direc-

An Introduction to Reference Services in Academic Libraries
© 2006 by The Haworth Press, Inc. All rights reserved.
doi:10.1300/5634_09

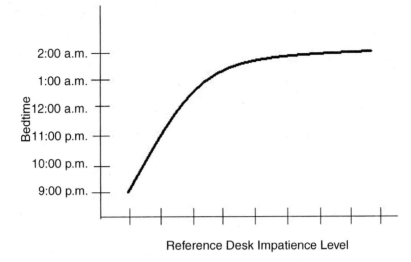

FIGURE C9.1. Badlow's Curve of Appropriate Bedtimes for Reference Staff

tionless, bookish, and lazy, probably a social outcast with longish limp hair, brown and dull. His elbows are scarred because he imagines he is a decent Roller Blader, but is not. He wears black Keds with red laces and 1950s-style horn-rimmed glasses, which he believes make him look intelligent and worldly. He keeps bodybuilding magazines hidden in his dorm room, but quickly hides them and picks up Dorothy Parker when his roommate, Ray, comes walking down the hall.

Of course, a new reference librarian will not be able to make these deductions right away. But after seeing one or two classes through to graduation, this level of insight is unavoidable (see Figure C9.2).

PROFESSORS EXPECTING MIRACLES

Another recurring theme of the college reference world is the "professor expecting miracles." He or she calls on Tuesday at 4:30 p.m. asking that a course packet of twenty-three articles be ready for his or her students before Wednesday's opening bell. Or he or she will show up at the desk frantic to verify an obscure citation, a letter from Kant to Richardson, never published but rumored to be in an uncataloged

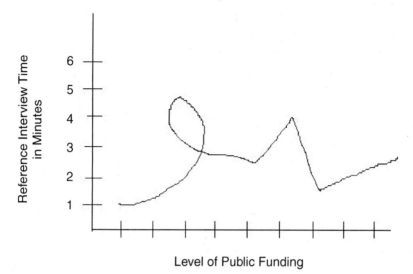

FIGURE C9.2. Bathsalt's Conundrum

box of letters at the Universität Tubingen; his or her final dissertation extension is, of course, expiring on Sunday. Many novices have fallen under the weight of the "professor expecting miracles," many tears shed. Experienced librarians know, however, to give such cases over to tenured librarians who have more latitude to be frank in their analysis of the professor and his or her current straits.

UNDERGRADUATE EXPECTATIONS

Undergraduates, too, carry fantasies about what librarians may be able to do. Toward the end of every fall semester we receive at least one request to "Send me everything you have on chemistry!" And every year the librarians are tempted to comply.

"Can I bring my Anthro 101 class to the library tomorrow afternoon and have you show them how to do research?" never fails to send chills through the novice and make him or her question whether serial check-in might be a more suitable career.

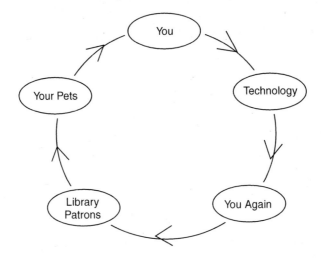

FIGURE C9.3. Library Life Cycle, Proposed by Dr. Francis Snorkul, 1978

Technical questions abound, like "My scroll lock isn't working" or "What does the escape key do?" which assumes that the reference librarian and Mr. Gates were separated at birth. Or the philosophical questions like "Is it fair to refuse to give extensions on papers?" and "Why do I always wait until the last minute?" which are easily disposed of by the seasoned professional (Figure C9.3).

Our staff recommends collecting such queries, along with the responses, in three-ring binders, categorized for the general subject of the question. In this way, one generation of librarians can pass its wisdom to the next. After all, for "down the hall and to the left," one shouldn't have to reinvent the wheel.

EXERCISES

1. Summarize this case study, stating the main points for a classmate or co-worker who knows very little about the subject or has not read the case study. Relate this case study to your experience as a student, employee, or customer.
2. Rewrite the summary for a different audience (expert in the field, college administrator, fund-raiser).

3. With a classmate or co-worker, role-play the case study, with one person playing the author, and the other person asking the author about his or her purpose, motivations, main points, evidence, conclusions, etc.
4. Do you agree or disagree with the main points of the case study? Do you base this on prior knowledge, opinion, author's arguments, cited evidence, intuition, or a combination of these elements? Does humor help highlight concepts?
5. Find one scholarly, authoritative source (book or article) that supports or refutes the main points of this case study. Detail the sources consulted and the search terms used.
6. Based on the evidence presented in the preceding case study, what do you think are the most significant challenges facing academic librarians dealing with common reference questions or patterns of behavior?

Case Study 10

Models for Measuring and Evaluating Reference Costs

Matthew R. Marsteller
Susan Ware

INTRODUCTION

This chapter uses case studies and two Web-based digital reference cost calculators to illustrate the choices and challenges involved in measuring the cost of offering a digital reference service. The models are interactive and reusable for any number of cost formulations. Case studies provide practical scenarios designed to show the strengths and limitations of the cost models. Exercises are included to clarify concepts and challenge readers to think critically about service issues.

As library collections become more digital, the need to develop, staff, and maintain Web-based reference service points increases. Many libraries have expanded reference services to online users by experimenting with service delivery through chat, e-mail, instant messaging, and mobile phone text messaging. In addition, with fiscal responsibilities in mind, academic libraries may be faced with shrinking reference budgets or a demand for greater accountability from their funding sources. In pursuit of both cost savings and improved service, libraries may change service hours and staffing patterns, enter into consortial staffing agreements, outsource services, and monitor the success of their transactions. A widely used technique for reference transaction cost studies is described as follows, followed by case studies that illustrate how overall costs change as software costs, service hours, staffing, and quality are adjusted.

An Introduction to Reference Services in Academic Libraries
© 2006 by The Haworth Press, Inc. All rights reserved.
doi:10.1300/5634_10

REFERENCE SERVICE COST STUDIES

Reference cost studies conducted by academic libraries frequently seek to measure the costs and efficiencies of staffing reference service points. Managers often use these data to make decisions about the number and placement of service points, the hours of service, and the level of staffing. One approach to measuring service cost is to calculate a unit cost, and then multiply that cost by the number of times the unit is performed. The typical unit cost measured is the cost of a single reference transaction. By multiplying the unit cost of an average reference transaction by the number of reference transactions handled in one month (or one year or whatever time span is desired), the cost of reference transactions per unit of time is measured. The key is to determine the average length of time taken to complete a reference transaction. This has proven to be rather difficult to do in face-to-face reference, telephone reference, and e-mail reference. The major difficulty has been the ability of the reference librarian to measure the length of the transaction accurately. What happens during a busy period at the reference desk? What happens when a librarian gets one patron started on a quest for information, starts with a second patron, and then checks up on the progress of both patrons? How do you measure transaction length when the librarian spends parts of several days answering a difficult reference question? How is transaction length measured when one is interrupted frequently while working on a reference question? In these cases, the librarian must estimate the time devoted to the questions or an independent observer must be employed to time the transactions. In addition, conducting an accurate daily count with measurement of transaction lengths is so labor intensive that, most often, the best that can be achieved is a representative sample.

REFERENCE TRANSACTION LOGS

With sophisticated synchronous chat reference software, reference transaction logs can be generated to maintain a record of the duration of each transaction and a verbatim transcript. For the first time in reference service, very accurate measurements can be made under controlled conditions. However, one shortcoming of today's software packages is their inability to report when a librarian handles questions from more than one patron at a time. During high traffic times, one librarian may toggle between two or three patrons who may ask for help in rapid succession.

If fairly accurate measurements can be made of the duration of each reference transaction, there may be a temptation to compare librarians for efficiency. This would be quite unfair and could lead to poor service if librarians, worried about keeping their transactions short, conduct less than adequate reference interviews in an attempt to appear more efficient. When librarians encounter patrons who are text messaging through a cell phone, have limited typing skills, or are using a slow modem, delays are inevitable. These delays could be identified as environmental challenges. Reference managers must not overlook environmental challenges in their pursuit of cost efficiencies.

INTERACTIVE DIGITAL REFERENCE COST MODELS

The Synchronous Digital Reference Cost Calculator (http://www.andrew.cmu.edu/user/matthewm/vrd2003/DigRefCostModel.html) uses a spreadsheet to calculate direct and indirect costs associated with providing digital reference services including labor, software, attendance at committee meetings, administration, and facilities maintenance. Users enter numeric information (service hours, service points, transactions, length of transactions, etc.) to estimate costs per year. Footnotes at the bottom of the model's Web page explain the underlying details of the calculations. Many of the variables used in the calculator are also relevant to a traditional reference desk setting.

SPECIFIC CASES

Case Study A: Expanded Hours and Increased Software Costs

Carnegie Mellon expanded its chat reference service from twenty to thirty-two hours per week, with the expectation that the expanded service would receive eighty-eight questions per month (up from an actual average of fifty-five questions per month). At the same time, the software costs for Carnegie Mellon increased from $4,200 per year to $5,040 per year. The default settings of the Synchronous Digital Reference Cost Calculator represent the old service parameter measurements. Figure C10.1 shows the default settings for the calculator.

Figure C10.2 shows the Synchronous Digital Reference Cost Calculator with the service parameters and software costs changed. The numbers of hours of service per week, the average number of reference transactions per month, and the cost of software per year per seat have been altered as indicated. Note that the maximum reference transactions per month that the model can handle have gone up to 832 questions per month. This is due to the expanded hours. In retrospect, it is unlikely that the heavy traffic model would ever be used—the number of service points would typically be increased before the traffic level approached the caution level. The cost of software per minute of service may be surprising. The increase in software costs had less of an impact on the per-minute cost than the increased use of the software from twenty to thirty-two hours per week—thus, the cost of software per minute of service went down. Carnegie Mellon increased service availability by 60 percent. Note that this drives up the cost of providing the service, but Carnegie Mellon University Libraries is more concerned with making its services available to its user community at the point and time of need.

Caution: if your "Reference transactions per month" are greater than the number to the right, then you need to be using the heavy traffic model (see box below).	520	Cost of software per year per seat	4,200.00
Number of hours of service per week	20	Cost of software per year	4,200.00
Number of service points	1	Cost of software per minute of service	0.07
Average work week in hours	37	Mean salary for librarians per hour	20.94
		Mean salary for librarians per minute	0.45
Average length of reference transaction in minutes	10	Estimated labor cost per reference transaction	4.49
Reference transactions per month	55	Estimated total compensation per reference transaction (with fringe benefits)	6.26
		Estimated total labor compensation per month	344.42
		Estimated total labor compensation per year	3,804.61
Number of committee/task force/work group meetings per year	3		
Average meeting attendance	4	Estimated total cost per year	8,417.89
Labor cost of meetings (assuming 1 hour meetings) per year	223.26		
		Estimated total cost per year with facility and administrative costs included	13,131.91

☑ Automatic recalculation   [Recalculate]

FIGURE C10.1. Default Settings of the Synchronous Digital Reference Cost Calculator

Caution: if your "Reference transactions per month" are greater than the number to the right, then you need to be using the heavy traffic model (see link below).	832	Cost of software per year per seat	5,040.00
Number of hours of service per week	32	Cost of software per year	5,040.00
Number of service points	1	Cost of software per minute of service	0.05
Average workweek in hours	37	Mean salary for librarians per hour	20.94
		Mean salary for librarians per minute	0.45
Average length of reference transaction in minutes	10	Estimated labor cost per reference transaction	4.49
Reference transactions per month	68	Estimated total compensation per reference transaction (with fringe benefits)	8.26
		Estimated total labor compensation per month	651.07
		Estimated total labor compensation per year	8,231.57
Number of committee/task force/work group meetings per year	3		
Average meeting attendance	4	Estimated total cost per year	11,994.65
Labor cost of meetings (assuming 1 hour meetings) per year	223.28		
		Estimated total cost per year with facility and administrative costs included	18,087.65

☑ Automatic recalculation [Recalculate]

FIGURE C10.2. Estimate of New Costs for Carnegie Mellon

The use of the model for digital reference at Carnegie Mellon does not illustrate the entire situation. Although the service was expanded by twelve hours, the new hours provided by librarians also cover other types of reference service. The original twenty hours of chat reference service are still being provided by librarians who do not handle other reference service. At the same time, other types of reference service were curtailed by four hours per week at three service points for a total of twelve hours. It is legitimate to calculate the increased costs of providing synchronous digital reference service, but overall reference service costs are not much different. Carnegie Mellon's goal was to provide service hours that would receive more reference traffic. When costs per transaction are measured, more traffic at any type of reference desk drives up the cost of the service.

Case Study B: Cost Estimate for a Small Academic Library

The true test of a model comes from its application in an entirely new situation. In a hypothetical case of synchronous digital reference at a small college library, the hourly pay rate might be somewhat above or below the national average. The model can accommodate a lower rate of twenty dollars per hour, lighter traffic (forty questions per month), a different length of time per transaction (fifteen minutes), a different annual software cost, etc. If this small college used an after-hours service to provide 24/7 coverage, though, this situation cannot be handled easily by the model. The typical arrangement calls for a set amount of cost-per-reference transaction provided by the after-hours service. The cost could be included with the software cost, but it would be more useful to improve the model. Figure C10.3 shows the model being used for a cost estimate for the small college library.

Case Study C: Cost of Failed Transactions

As a measure of quality control, transcripts of digital reference sessions can be assessed against locally determined criteria to measure success. The success of a transaction might be judged by the accuracy of the answer, thoroughness of the reference interview, or quality of the interpersonal interaction. Success might also be judged by the availability of needed resources or the technical quality of software. In addition, an arbitrary monetary cost can be assigned to failed transactions to represent the level of concern for ineffective service that might result in a patron's frustration, time wasted, or academic failure. With this in mind, a revised Synchronous Digital Reference Cost Effectiveness Calculator was created to include entries for the aver-

FIGURE C10.3. Cost Estimate for a Small College Library

age number of failed transactions and a penalty fee for failed transactions (see Figure C10.4). The revised model is available at http://www.andrew.cmu.edu/user/matthewm/DigRefCostEffModel.html.

Case C is a hypothetical case of synchronous digital reference at a university that offers online degree programs to students worldwide. Enrollments are high and most courses have rigorous research demands. Quality digital reference service is very important to these programs because most enrolled students do not have access to the physical facilities of the main library. To maintain quality control, the library staff reviews a sample of the session transcripts each month and makes three assessments: one for the quality of the transaction, one for the availability of needed resources, and one for the technical stability of the software. They also set their performance goal high (80 percent) and set the penalty fee for a failed transaction at twice the cost of a successful transaction. The library's goal is to keep the total labor cost for failed transactions per year to a maximum of 20 percent of the cost of successful transactions per year.

The Synchronous Digital Reference Cost Effectiveness Calculator can accommodate the three assessments. In Figure C10.5, note that the cost of a successful transaction is determined with the following service parameters: 60 hours of service per week, 1 service point, average length of transaction is 10 minutes, average number of transac-

Number of hours of service per week*	33	Mean salary for librarian per hour***	26.93	
Number of service points*	1	Mean salary for librarian per minute	0.45	
Average length of reference transaction in minutes*	10	Estimated salary per reference transaction	4.49	
Average number of reference transactions per month (Note: consult numbers about only reflect the number of transactions handled by their library)*	88	Estimated total labor cost per reference transaction (salary with fringe benefits)	8.95	
		Estimated total labor cost per month	550.49	
		Estimated total labor cost per year	6,315.37	
Average number of failed reference transactions per month*	5	Estimated total labor cost for failed transactions per year (with penalty fee, if applied)	672.96	
Penalty fee per failed reference transaction****	3.00	Estimated total labor cost for successful transactions per year	5,995.45	
Number of internal reference committee/task force/work group meetings per year*	3			
Average meeting attendance*	4	Consortium fee for the service per year*	800.00	
Labor cost of meetings (assuming 1 hour meetings) per year	323.53	After hours service cost per year*	0.000.00	
Cost of software per year per seat*	5,000.00	Estimated total cost per year	10,470.79	
Cost of software per year	6,000.00	Facility & Administrative cost (Percentage above)*	95%	
Cost of software per minute of service	0.05	Estimated total cost per year with Facility and Administrative cost included	29,808.91	

FIGURE C10.4. Revised

Number of hours of service per week[*]	60	Mean salary for librarians per hour[***]	26.96
Number of service points[*]	1	Mean salary for librarians per minute	0.45
Average length of reference transaction in minutes[*]	10	Estimated salary per reference transaction	4.49
Average number of reference transactions per month [Note: consortia members should only reflect the number of transactions handled by their library][*]	300	Estimated total labor cost per reference transaction (salary with fringe benefits)	6.35
		Estimated total labor cost per month	1,802.96
		Estimated total labor cost per year	21,529.34
Average number of failed reference transactions per month[*]	0	Estimated total labor cost for failed transactions per year (with penalty fee, if applied)	0.00
Penalty fee per failed reference transaction[*] [**]	0.00	Estimated total labor cost for successful transactions per year	21,529.34
Number of internal reference committee/task force/work group meetings per year[*]	8		
Average meeting attendance[*]	12	Consortium fee for the service per year[*]	0.00
Labor cost of meetings (assuming 1 hour meetings) per year	3,966.58	After hours service cost per year[*]	0.00
Cost of software per year per seat[*]	5,000.00	Estimated total cost per year	30,129.90
Cost of software per year	5,000.00	Facility & Administrative cost (Percentage used)[*]	56%
Cost of software per minute of service	0.09	Estimated total cost per year with Facility and Administrative cost included	47,105.60

☑ Amounts rounded to [Recalculate]

FIGURE C10.5. Estimated Cost per Successful Transaction with No Failed Transactions

tions per month is 300, there are no failed transactions, software cost per year is $5,000, and mean per-hour salary for librarians is $26.96. The estimated total labor cost per successful transaction per year is $6.35 and the estimated total labor cost per year is $21,529.34.

However, if the average number of failed reference transactions per month is 20 (6.67 percent of the average number of reference transactions per month), the penalty for each failed transaction is $12.70 (2 × $6.35), according to the local performance standard. In Figure C10.6, note that the estimated total labor cost of failed transactions per year is $4,307.44. This amount is more than 20 percent of the estimated total labor cost of successful transactions per year ($20,094.05), so the library's goal has been narrowly missed. Notice that the changes for the estimated total labor cost for failed transactions per year (with penalty fee, if applied) occur only in that cell, they do not affect real costs. Inspired by this challenge to meet or surpass its goal, the library staff can work to improve performance by enhancing reference skills, adding resources to the collection to meet the demonstrated need, or troubleshooting software problems more efficiently.

Number of hours of service per week"	60	Mean salary for librarians per hour" ""		26.98
Number of service points"	1	Mean salary for librarians per minute		0.45
Average length of reference transaction in minutes"	10	Estimated salary per reference transaction		4.49
Average number of reference transactions per month (Note: consortia members should only reflect the number of transactions handled by their library)"	300	Estimated total labor cost per reference transaction (salary with fringe benefits)		6.35
		Estimated total labor cost per month		1,902.95
		Estimated total labor cost per year		21,929.34
Average number of failed reference transactions per month"	30	Estimated total labor cost for failed transactions per year (with penalty fee, if applied)	4,307.44	
Penalty fee per failed reference transaction" ""	12.70	Estimated total labor cost for successful transactions per year	30,184.05	
Number of internal reference committee/task force/work group meetings per year"	6			
Average meeting attendance"	17	Consortium fee for the service per year"		0.00
Labor cost of meetings (assuming 1 hour meetings) per year	3,586.56	After-hours service cost per year"		0.00
Cost of software per year per seat"	5,000.00	Estimated total cost per year		30,126.90
Cost of software per year	5,000.00	Facility & Administrative cost (Percentage used)"		56%
Cost of software per minute of service	0.03	Estimated total cost per year with Facility and Administrative cost included		47,106.60

FIGURE C10.6. Estimated Cost for Failed Transactions per Year

CONCLUSION

Note that other simple improvements have been incorporated into the Synchronous Digital Reference Cost Effectiveness Calculator. The revised model accounts for the cost of an after-hours service and a consortium fee while accounting for the consortium member providing the labor for questions that only its library answers.

The use of an interactive model by multiple types of libraries can provide improved and readily available cost estimates for synchronous digital reference services. At the same time, it can make a useful educational tool by enhancing the understanding of the challenges faced by practicing librarians.

It is hoped that use of the Synchronous Digital Reference Cost Effectiveness Calculator, coupled with feedback on its successes and shortcomings, will result in ideas for improvement. Some feedback has already been received. Allocated costs for funds spent on the collections, office supplies, or for the time spent on the development of Web-based user guides, are examples of problems proving difficult to incorporate into the model. Why should the model be limited to just analyzing costs?

Perhaps an estimation of the benefits of a service could be added in the future. Persistence, creativity, and participation of the library community in the improvement of the model should garner further success.

Reviews of the Literature

Abels, Eileen, G. Improving Reference Service Cost Studies. *Library & Information Science Research* 19(1997): 135-152.

American Library Association. *The Reference Assessment Manual.* Ann Arbor, MI: Pierian Press, 1995.

Murfin, M.E. Cost Analysis of Library Reference Services. *Advances in Library Administration and Organization* 11(1993): 1-36.

Measuring Benefits and Effectiveness

Braunstein, Yale M. Costs and Benefits of Library Information: The Users Point of View. *Library Trends* 28(1979): 79-87.

Harless, David W. and Allen, Frank R. Using the Contingent Valuation Method to Measure Patron Benefits of Reference Desk Service in an Academic Library. *College & Research Libraries* 60(January 1999): 56-69.

Kuhlman, James R. On the Economics of Reference Service: Toward a Heuristic Model for an Uncertain World. *Reference Librarian* 49/50(1995): 25-43.

McClure, Charles. Output Measures, Unobtrusive Testing, and Assessing the Quality of Reference Services. *Reference Librarian* 11(1984): 215-333.

Orr, R.H. Measuring the Goodness of Library Services: A General Framework for Considering Quantitative Measures. *Journal of Documentation* 29(1973): 315-332.

Powell, Ronald R. Impact Assessment of University Libraries: A Consideration of Issues and Research Methodologies. *Library & Information Science Research* 14 (July/September 1992): 245-257.

Radcliff, Carolyn J. and Schloman, Barbara F. Using the Wisconsin-Ohio Reference Evaluation Program. (Case Study 3.1). In Danny P. Wallace and Connie Van Fleet (Eds.), *Library Evaluation: A Casebook and Can-Do Guide.* Englewood, CO: Libraries Unlimited, Inc., 2001.

Saracevic, Tefko and Kantor, Paul B. Studying the Value of Library and Information Services. Part II. Methodology and Taxonomy. *Journal of the American Society for Information Science* 48(1997): 543-563.

Measuring Digital Reference Cost and Quality

Gross, Melissa, McClure, Charles R., and Lankes, R. David. *Assessing Quality in Digital Reference Services: Overview of Key Literature on Digital Reference.* Information Institute of Syracuse, School of Information Studies; School of Information Studies, Information Use Management and Policy Institute, Florida State University, 2001.

Lankes, R. David, Gross, Melissa, and McClure, Charles. Cost, Statistics, Measures, and Standards for Digital Reference Services: A Preliminary View. *Library Trends* 51 (Winter 2003): 401-413.

McClure, Charles R., Lankes, R. David, Gross, Melissa, and Choltco-Devlin, Beverly. *Statistics, Measures, and Quality Standards for Assessing Digital Reference Library Services: Guidelines and Procedures.* Information Institute of Syracuse, School of Information Studies; School of Information Studies, Information Use Management and Policy Institute, Florida State University, 2002.

Radford, Marie L. In Synch: Evaluating Chat Reference Transcripts. *Virtual Reference Desk Conference Proceedings* (2003). Available at http://www.vrd2003.org/proceedings/presentation.cfm?PID=231. Accessed August 1, 2005.

White, Marilyn D., Abels, Eileen G., and Kaske, Neal. Evaluation of Chat Reference Service Quality, Pilot Study. *D-Lib Magazine* 9(2) (2003). Available at http://www.dlib.org/dlib/february03/white/02white.html. Accessed August 1, 2005.

EXERCISES

1. Summarize this case study, stating the main points for a classmate or co-worker who knows very little about the subject or who has not read the case study. Relate this case study to your experience as a student, employee, or customer.

2. Rewrite the summary for a different audience (expert in the field, college administrator, fund-raiser).

3. With a classmate or co-worker, role-play the case study, with one person playing the author, and the other person asking the author about his or her purpose, motivations, main points, evidence, conclusions, etc.

4. Do you agree or disagree with the main points of the case study? Do you base this on prior knowledge, opinion, authors; arguments, cited evidence, intuition, or a combination of these elements?

5. Find two scholarly, authoritative sources (books or articles) that support or refute the main points of this case study. Detail the sources consulted and the search terms used.

6. Based on the evidence presented in the preceding case study, what do you think are the most significant challenges facing academic librarians interested in marketing traditional or virtual reference services? Compare the evidence presented in this case study with Case Study 5.

7. Develop three to five interview questions that could be used to interview a practicing academic librarian about his or her experience using cost models with various library services.

8. Write a one-page memorandum to a hypothetical library supervisor justifying why a specific academic library should implement, continue, or discontinue virtual reference services.

Case Study 11

Customer Survey

Miron Stenche

INTRODUCTION

Darkmound University offers a seven-year undeclared baccalaure-ate program to underachieving, upper-middle-class students in north-eastern New York State. The university has two master's programs: library science and animal husbandry. Both programs should be fully accredited within the next five to ten years.

OBJECTIVE

At the start of the fall 2003 semester, the Fraught Memorial Library undertook a survey of customer needs which would form the basis of a new collection development policy (CDP). The CDP has not been rewritten since 1971 and uses idioms such as "freaks" to describe certain groups of students, and leaned strongly toward books on meditation, third-world revolution, and hitchhiking, while pointedly ignoring standard history and mathematics texts. Clearly, a rewrite of the CDP was overdue and staff recognized that a customer needs survey was the place to start.

METHOD

The library director appointed a task force of four professional reference librarians to devise a questionnaire and conduct customer in-

An Introduction to Reference Services in Academic Libraries
© 2006 by The Haworth Press, Inc. All rights reserved.
doi:10.1300/5634_11

terviews. When the technical services librarians protested their exclusion from the process, the library director outsourced technical services thus averting a serious morale problem.

The task force began its work by searching for pertinent literature on the subject of library customer needs surveys. When indexes for *National Geographic, Sports Illustrated,* and *Vintage Guitars* turned up no significant references, the task force realized that such a study would be the first of its kind. The task force then went through a period of intense discussion and disagreement until they reached consensus that Isabelle would be exempt from taking minutes, due to her poor spelling.

By late October 2001, staff had agreed on ten questions that would elicit information necessary to guide a revision of the CDP. Five of these questions would be addressed to students, five to teaching staff:

Students

1. Do you plan to graduate from Darkmound University?
2. Have any of your previous classes involved reading?
3. Are your parents in a position to endow the Darkmound University Library?
4. Are you sure?
5. What is your favorite color?

Teachers

1. Are your classes geared toward a particular subject?
   a. Do any of the classes you teach involve reading?
   b. Are you squeamish about violating "fair use" copyright provisions?
   c. Have you ever visited the Fraught Library? (modernish building next to stadium)
   d. What is your favorite color?

Task force members conducted interviews over winter break, when staff could be spared from the reference and circulation desks.

RESULTS

Because of the unfortunate timing of the interviews, only three students and four faculty were available for the survey. Survey results, therefore, cannot be considered "conclusive." Although the task force found it interesting that "blue" was not listed as a favorite color in its sampling, they ultimately recommended to the library director that staff move ahead drafting the CDP with little or no insight into student and faculty preferences.

CONCLUSION

In the four years since the completion of the survey, the CDP rewrite has progressed just slightly beyond the "outline" stage. This Fraught Memorial Library case study should serve as a cautionary tale to other, primarily undergraduate institutions. Even the most clever and thoughtful surveys can fail if that survey is conducted when students and faculty are not on campus. However, one should balance that with the drastically reduced time necessary for the survey results to be tabulated.

EXERCISES

1. Summarize this case study, stating the main points for a classmate or co-worker who knows very little about the subject or who has not read the case study. Relate this case study to your experience as a student, employee, or customer.
2. Rewrite the summary for a different audience (expert in the field, college administrator, fund-raiser).
3. With a classmate or co-worker, role-play the case study, with one person playing the author, and the other person asking the author about his or her purpose, motivations, main points, evidence, conclusions, etc.
4. Do you agree or disagree with the main points of the case study? Do you base this on prior knowledge, opinion, author's arguments, cited evidence, intuition, or a combination of these elements? Does humor help highlight important concepts?

5. Find one scholarly, authoritative source (book or article) that supports or refutes the main points of this case study. Detail the sources consulted and the search terms used.
6. Based on the evidence presented in the preceding case study, how do you think academic librarians should go about developing or revising a collection development policy?

PART II:
ESSAYS

Essay 1

The Diverse Librarian

Paula M. Smith

Diversity is one of those topics that is so broad it is difficult to know where to enter the conversation. At its essence, it seems to attempt to nullify the ills of the world, by promoting inclusion as a solution to historical attempts to exclude. It seeks a systematic approach to healing, instead of just throwing open the doors and allowing the excluded to make themselves at home. This notion maintains that once in the door, you are a guest, not a resident. What I mean is that there is an inherent expectation in diversity to assimilate: you may bring your culture but not too much of it.

Despite the involvement of librarians of color in the information profession since the early 1800s, it is only in the past thirty years that diversity in the profession has been acknowledged and given credence. Although a clear meaning of diversity has been elusive, it has generally encompassed race, ethnicity, and sexual orientation. As the profession struggles for societal relevance, the recruitment and retention of new librarians has been emphasized, especially of those candidates representing a difference from the majority. Historically, librarianship sought to provide a homogenous approach to the stewardship of information, neither defining a place nor acknowledging the need for ideas contrary to a mainstream point of view. In more recent times, the profession has begun to pave the way in earnest toward achieving a workforce and library collections that both represent and reflect the populations served.

Since the 1960s, librarians of color have been seeking a voice in librarianship. Leading the charge has been Dr. E. J. Josey, the first African-American president of the American Library Association

An Introduction to Reference Services in Academic Libraries
© 2006 by The Haworth Press, Inc. All rights reserved.
doi:10.1300/5634_12

(ALA), keeping the issue of diversity at the forefront of ALA's agenda. If not for his continued efforts to spotlight minority concerns prior to and during his tenure as president, the organizations and initiatives dedicated to increasing the numbers of the underrepresented would not exist. Dr. Josey has been a tireless pioneer and champion of diversity in libraries. From his demand in the 1960s that ALA deny membership and disassociate itself from library organizations supportive of segregation in the profession,[1] to the founding of the Black Caucus of the American Library Association in the 1970s, which spawned the multicultural library organizations that serve other race and ethnic minorities today,[2] Dr. Josey continues to be the conscience of the profession. He addresses the inequity in the ranks of library administration and faculty. His hard work and dedication are underlying factors for the existence of the Office for Diversity within ALA and the Spectrum Initiative program, which it administers. The Spectrum program consists of scholarships, fund-raising, recruitment, mentoring, leadership, and professional development for people of color to enter the library profession.

Today, "diversity is one of the five areas adopted by the American Library Association to fulfill its mission of providing the highest quality library and information services for all people."[3] Fundamentally, it is interwoven throughout much of the committee work performed within ALA and other library organizations. Although much of this reform in librarianship is driven by an aging staff, technological innovation, and a demographic shift, it is also recognized that having diverse library employees facilitates a stronger profession that is better able to address the needs of its constituency. Now that diversity is at the forefront of ALA issues, efforts to achieve diversity in librarianship have materialized in many forms, from conferences to leadership institutes, from internships to residency fellowships, yet the attempts to attract and retain candidates of color have been less than successful.

Inherently, libraries are information repositories for the history and traditions that underlie each of our cultural identities. The purpose of libraries is to provide diverse communities with intellectual stimulation and cultural enrichment, while being a conduit for lifelong learning. In order to support a welcoming environment, and to provide service to its constituencies, the library has sought to broaden its base and diversify its workforce. However, in spite of the greater emphasis to diversify the rank and file of libraries in play, library culture in many ways has remained the same. With few persons of color in the lower echelons of libraries, even fewer have appointments in library schools or in the administration of the profession's governing bodies. To achieve diversity goals of representing and reflecting libraries' populations, employing strategies that include a top-down and bottom-up approach seem warranted. It is not enough to fund programs to gain access to the entry levels of the profession—creative ways must be employed to expand access at all levels.

In the end, the nature of diversity is not only about having persons of color, ethnicity, or other special categories included in the library spectrum; it is welcoming the unique and different perspectives delivered by varied voices. It is acknowledging the similarities, as often as the differences. In my experience, librarians symbolizing "a difference" to the profession have entered librarianship for the same reason as those who have held the majority representation. Their goals also include providing information and serving their communities, while expecting their ideas to be heard, acknowledged, and implemented. I have yet to hear a librarian who does not want to participate in professional development and partake in opportunities for growth and promotion. As we celebrate our small victory of increased participation and funding for the underrepresented we must keep in mind that only a narrow path has been paved and it requires all of our efforts to reach back for the many.

NOTES

1. Josey, E. J. and Abdullahi, Ibrahim. Why Diversity in American Libraries. *Library Management* 23(1/2) (2002): 10-16.
2. Yamashita, Kenneth A. History of APALA and its Founders. *Library Trends* 49(Summer) (2000): 88-108.
3. American Library Association. *Diversity.* 2004. Available at http://www.ala.org/Template.cfm?Section=diversityb. Accessed August 1, 2005.

EXERCISES

1. Summarize this essay, stating the main points for a classmate or co-worker who knows very little about the subject or who has

not read the case study. Relate this essay to your experience as a student, employee, or customer.

2. Rewrite the summary for a different audience (expert in the field, college administrator, fund-raiser).

3. With a classmate or co-worker, role-play the essay, with one person playing the author, and the other person asking the author about his or her purpose, motivations, main points, evidence, conclusions, etc.

4. Do you agree or disagree with the main points of this essay? Do you base this on prior knowledge, opinion, author's arguments, cited evidence, intuition, or a combination of these elements?

5. Find two scholarly, authoritative sources (books or articles) that support or refute the main points of this essay. Detail the sources consulted and the search terms used.

6. Based on this essay, what do you think are the most significant challenges facing academic librarians interested in diversifying library education and practice?

7. Develop three to five interview questions that could be used to interview a practicing academic librarian about his or her experience promoting diversity in the library workplace.

Essay 2

Academic Librarian As the Rodney Dangerfield of University Faculty: "I Get No Respect"

Tammy S. Guerrero

My name is Tammy Guerrero. I am an academic librarian. I get no respect. I have worked hard to achieve the status that I have at the university, but I get no respect. Let me explain. Many academic librarians have faculty status. Many are in tenure-track positions. I am no exception. I hold a master's degree in library science from Indiana University. I worked very hard to get that degree. I commuted from northwest Indiana to Indianapolis, which is over four hours, round trip. I did this every Friday for two years. I did this while working full-time, raising three children, managing a household, etc. It was tough, but I persevered. In December 2001, all this paid off when I was awarded my degree. I was appointed the academic librarian position in January 2002.

This essay is for those of you brave souls entering into the wonderful world of librarianship. Don't get me wrong. I love being a librarian. I love my career. I have no regrets. My point is . . . we get no respect. When you complete your degree and get a job in a library, be prepared to hear comments like, "You need a master's degree to be a librarian?" That is the most popular one. If you become an academic librarian, be prepared to have to defend your position constantly with the "real faculty." This is where the irony comes into play. We go to school, we get a master's degree, we land a great job as an academic librarian. We are in a tenure-track position, or "chasing tenure" as the "real faculty" like to call it. We do book reviews, we publish in schol-

An Introduction to Reference Services in Academic Libraries
© 2006 by The Haworth Press, Inc. All rights reserved.
doi:10.1300/5634_13

arly journals within our field, we present papers at national and international conferences, and we sit on university committees. Oh, I forgot one minor detail. We do all this while working forty-hour weeks. Sometimes we work more. In my case, in addition to all this, I manage a unit, which includes scheduling and supervising employees.

Let's get back to the issue of respect. Here's my theory on why we get little to none. First of all, as I stated earlier, most teaching faculty or "real faculty" don't realize that academic librarians have faculty rank. In my case, I'm hit with it even more so, because I was part of our library's clerical support team for fifteen years before I got my MLS and got appointed to my faculty position. I also got my undergraduate degree here, so when professors see me, they either think "student" or "clerical staff." They don't think of me as "faculty." I've had to work very hard to reeducate people. It's an honest misconception that can't be helped. What really toots my flute is when you explain to these faculty members that you, too, are faculty and they still disrespect you. We hear comments like, "Well, why are you on this committee? I thought it only consisted of *real faculty.*" Or, how about this one, "Oh, they let *librarians* serve on committees too?" All these comments are rude and condescending, but we continue to hear them. The final blow is the fact that our salaries are substantially lower than classroom faculty. That's just icing on the cake!

Another reason we get no respect from "teaching faculty" is because librarians are generally considered to be their servants. Our jobs are service oriented, because we are constantly helping someone, ordering something for someone, or delivering something to someone. There are a few loyal faculty members who use the library regularly and respect the faculty positions we hold. They agree that we should be here, should have faculty rank, and deserve respect. They are a small but brave bunch, and we love them.

Let's talk for a minute about why academic librarians deserve to be ranked among the faculty. First of all, we hold professional degrees. We have put in the time and logged the hours (and in my case, miles) to get to this point. Second, we do teach. Our instructional services librarian teaches over 100 instructional sessions per semester. For those of us who only hold instructional sessions occasionally, or not at all, we still teach. We are teaching one-on-one each and every day. When we sit down with patrons and show them how to use a database or the electronic catalog, we are teaching. Also, when an accreditation team comes to size up our university, I would assume that if the librarians are ranked as faculty, that makes our university that much more valuable. If you demand that your professional staff continue to educate themselves beyond their professional degree, I would also assume that you look that much better to an accreditation team. That is just my educated and slightly biased opinion.

What else do we do that gives us the right to hold faculty positions? We do extensive research in our fields. We contribute to our profession by publishing books, book chapters, articles, and essays in library-related journals. We read current journals in our field and review books in our field. We read other book reviews and select new books for our collections. In doing so, we are supporting the curriculum here at the university. We make sure that when a professor gives an assignment, and the students come here to research, we have an ample supply of books to support them. We weed out old and outdated material so that young scholars can come here and find the most recent ideas, opinions, and research being done in his or her field. We take surveys and ask reference patrons to evaluate our services so that we can better serve the university. We have established a strategic plan with a mission, values, and goals. We have biweekly staff meetings to ensure that we are on the right track to attain these goals. We collaborate with "real faculty" to find out what their needs are so that we can meet them. We attend and present at national and international conferences, keeping up with current trends and innovations. We purchase and maintain current technology, software, and equipment.

Let's talk about the schedules we work. Our library is open seventy-five hours per week during the regular semesters. This includes nights and weekends. We have recently broken ground on student housing. There are rumors wafting in the air that "the powers that be" will be asking us to extend our hours to accommodate these dorm-dwellers. Now, we have to cover seventy-five hours at the present time, and possibly more in the future. This means that when a "real faculty" member teaches his or her required amount of classes, and maybe hold office hours a couple of times a week, they can go home. They are done. We are here days, nights, weekends and not necessarily in that order. When we have staff picnics, academic breakfasts, service recognition luncheons, good-bye parties, and related festivities, we must go in shifts. We can't close the library down and go to these functions. We must take turns and always keep the library open.

Where is the justice here, I ask you? Couldn't I close my library down just this once and go across the street for a hot dog, ice cream cone, or perhaps a pancake with my co-workers? Why must the librarians suffer so? Why can't we rub elbows with the hoi polloi? Why can't we get to the party before all the cake is eaten? Haven't we earned that right? Why must we be ostracized? Why must we be the outcast, black sheep of academia? We're nice, really we are. We're helpful, and most important, we are loyal. You won't find a more loyal friend than a librarian. We are here for you. We're keeping the light on for you. We've gone to school, studied hard, and fought for scarce library jobs. We will chase down a reference question like a dog chasing a car. We will persevere, collaborate, sweat, and even pray until we find your answer. The answers are out there, and we won't rest until we find them. Another of our attributes is that we're corny. Some of us are downright funny. I can have an entire room in stitches when I give an instructional session. It is a talent that I didn't learn in library school. Librarians usually know all the corny jokes and we are not afraid to use them. If we don't know them all, we know where to find them.

All in all, I guess being an academic librarian is not so bad, even with the "Rodney Dangerfield" thing going on and all. We get to help people and that feels good. We are an elite bunch and we will never stop striving to get that much-deserved, long-overdue respect. As I often tell my sister, who is a nurse and has saved many lives, I may not be saving lives, but I am helping educate people who will eventually go on to be doctors and nurses who will be saving lives, and they will have me to thank.

So, for those of you who still want to be a librarian, I salute you. You have a brave soul, a kind heart, and a strong stomach.

EXERCISES

1. Summarize this essay, stating the main points for a classmate or co-worker who knows very little about the subject or who has not read the case study. Relate this essay to your experience as a student, employee, or customer.
2. Rewrite the summary for a different audience (expert in the field, college administrator, fund-raiser).

3. With a classmate or co-worker, role-play the essay, with one person playing the author, and the other person asking the author about his or her purpose, motivations, main points, evidence, conclusions, etc.
4. Do you agree or disagree with the main points of this essay? Do you base this on prior knowledge, opinion, author's arguments, cited evidence, intuition, or a combination of these elements?
5. Find two scholarly, authoritative sources (books or articles) that support or refute the main points of this essay. Detail the sources consulted and the search terms used.
6. Based on this essay, what do you think are the most significant challenges facing academic librarians who feel disrespected, marginalized, or underappreciated?
7. Develop three to five interview questions that could be used to interview an entry-level and a midcareer academic librarian about his or her experiences building mutual respect in an academic community. Would you ask them the same or different questions?

The Teaching Portfolio: Explaining What We Do So Well

Mark L. McCallon

INTRODUCTION

The role of reference services today has become more teaching centered than service centered. This can be seen especially in academic libraries where teaching is the primary responsibility of the reference librarian. The reference librarian partners with teaching faculty to improve pedagogical outcomes and serves as an expert guide in empowering students to retrieve, analyze, use, and create information. As academic libraries make a stronger commitment to teaching, an outlet needs to be provided for reference librarians to reflect upon the role of teaching in librarianship and document evidence of performance and improvement. Many colleges and universities today are using the teaching portfolio as a measurement tool to assess the teaching effectiveness of librarians who play a significant role in the instructional process.

WHAT IS THE TEACHING PORTFOLIO?

A teaching portfolio is a collection of documents and artifacts that describes teaching effectiveness and provides evidence of outstanding accomplishments in producing quality educational materials and assignments. The development of a portfolio involves the careful preparation and organization of ideas and evidence to present a convincing argument for effective teaching and instruction. For this reason, it

An Introduction to Reference Services in Academic Libraries
© 2006 by The Haworth Press, Inc. All rights reserved.
doi:10.1300/5634_14

is important to begin compiling potential documents early in one's career.

The format of the portfolio is as individualized as the creator. As academic librarianship represents a variety of disciplines, the portfolio represents an individual's growth as a professional. It is important to consider the audience that will be viewing the portfolio in deciding how it is organized. Seldin identifies several key sections that are part of many teaching portfolios and provides a step-by-step approach for arranging the portfolio around teaching-related activities.[1]

SUMMARY OF TEACHING RESPONSIBILITIES

A summary of teaching responsibilities serves as a thesis statement for the portfolio and a rationale for the inclusion of items in other sections of the portfolio. The summary can be simply a set of factual statements such as "bibliographic instruction for English and History classes," or it may include detailed information about teaching strategies, staff training, and faculty development seminars. The format of the summary can take the form of a vitae or resume, or it may be several paragraphs long.

In addition to a brief description of teaching responsibilities, this section also provides the opportunity to discuss the teaching methods and strategies used in bibliographic instruction that affected one's development as a teacher. Descriptions of instructional tools such as tours, pathfinders, online catalog searches, or Webliographies provide a context for evaluation of the evidence. It is helpful to include a reflective sentence or two about the integration of learning philosophy with practice. An example from the portfolio of Judith Arnold, reference librarian at Marshall University, illustrates this effectively:

> Active learning is very important in our instruction for freshmen and ESL students who may not have very extensive experience with the library facilities. They have a great need for beginning strategies and for a tour/orientation to the layout and location of services and resources. In the first session for ESL students each student uses the catalog to locate a book on a topic of interest. They record the call number and location on a slip of paper.

Each row is given a periodical. They practice using the library's online periodical list to look up the specific periodical that their row has been assigned to find its call number and location. In the second half of the session we take a short tour and return the items to the appropriate place.

STUDENT EVALUATION DATA

Student evaluation data also enhance the description of bibliographic instruction sessions. Types of data include responses to survey questions or quotes from students regarding knowledge gained from instruction. Craig Churchill, theological librarian at Abilene Christian University presents student evaluations of his freshman seminar instruction in this manner:

I have participated in teaching the Library component of U100 classes throughout my time at ACU, and the quality of my teaching has been affirmed by students, U100 teachers, and several of my colleagues in the library. . . . However, more concrete evidence of my teaching effectiveness in U100 classes is afforded by the library unit evaluations given to students after each session. For comparative purposes, I include survey results from the overall Library Unit Evaluations for 2001, along with survey responses from the U100 class components I taught. Here (Tables E3.1 and E3.2), I represent responses to two of the survey questions which are especially pertinent to classroom instruction in these settings.

TABLE E3.1. Library Unit Evaluation—Effective Use of Library Resources (Survey Question 6: Do you feel you can use library resources more effectively due to participating in the library unit?)

	Frequency	5 (definitely yes)	4	3	2	1
Overall Library U100	593	33.8%	32.8%	21.9%	6.5%	4.2%
Churchill Library U100	77	59.7%	27%	9%	3%	1%

TABLE E3.2. Library Unit Evaluation—Quality of Library Presentation (Survey Question 3: How would you rate the quality of the library presentation?)

Survey Group	Frequency	5 (Excellent)	4	3	2	1 (Poor)
Overall Library U100	598	33.8%	21.9%	21.9%	6.5%	4.2%
Churchill Library U100	77	59.7%	27%	9%	3%	1%

TEACHING PHILOSOPHY STATEMENT

An essential part of the portfolio is an essay that captures the individuality of a teacher. This can be a laborious task because it requires careful thought and personal reflection about the beliefs and values that support one's teaching effectiveness. In the context of the portfolio, the teaching philosophy is an opportunity to discuss why certain teaching methods and learning objects are used in the classroom to promote meaningful learning. It is also helpful to expand the philosophy statement to teaching situations outside of the classroom such as mentoring a new colleague or leading a research team and discuss how teaching and learning in those situations are similar to the classroom. The process of developing a teaching philosophy helps librarians become more aware of their strengths and weaknesses as they document their observations of the "learning environment" in different situations. The Appendix provides a worksheet for developing a teaching philosophy.

The format and length of the teaching philosophy can vary widely. One approach to writing the essay is to think about the different aspects of teaching in relation to institutional goals. How do librarians connect with various types of students? What is the librarian's role in the learning process? Another approach is to analyze how personal experiences and observations have influenced one's teaching. Exhibit E3.1 presents excerpts from two teaching philosophies that typify these approaches.

Because of the variety of formats for teaching philosophy statements, it is a good idea to ask colleagues and peers to read the philosophy statement to provide suggestions for improvement. It may be helpful to ask a colleague in another subject field to read the state-

EXHIBIT E3.1.
Teaching Philosophy Statement

Laura Baker
Government Documents Librarian
Abilene Christian University

Libraries have always been places of wonder to me. My earliest library memories involve being taken to the neighborhood branch of the public library and discovering the magic of books. That older building was wonderfully cramped. It had green shaded lamps in the reading room, a narrow twisting staircase, and shelves stuffed with books at the ready. Every title was a potential treasure waiting to be opened. That library may not have been designed with today's architectural aesthetics in mind, but I loved my visits there. I have no doubt that those early experiences shaped me today.

At first the library was a source of stories, but I soon found it was a source of information, too. I found out there was system in place and that if I learned how the system worked, I could find treasures to satisfy my wants and my needs. I watched the librarian as she helped people find answers to their questions, and I thought I would like to be able to do what she did.

Librarianship is an old profession. It has seen many innovations in technology and information formats. There are many different types of libraries, all with different purposes, but despite changes in *how* librarians work, the fundamentals of *why* we work remain remarkably unchanged.

Mark McCallon
Business Reference Librarian and Assistant Director
Abilene Christian University

In my service role as a reference librarian, I seek to facilitate making research and library instruction part of the total educational experience for the students, staff, and faculty. Our rapidly changing world of information demands that university patrons be prepared to utilize the various technologies and research techniques which will allow them to locate their needed information. This is best done by on-the-field work, taking time and placing energies into assisting individuals and classes in their specific areas of concern. . . .

Through collaboration with the classroom teachers and colleagues in my department, instructional programs are developed which bring greater awareness of computer databases that are available to students and faculty. These programs open up more opportunities for interaction with faculty and students on a group and individual level,

(continued)

(continued)

making it possible to personalize my instruction to the patrons' specific areas of concern. This builds not only their warehouse of knowledge and expertise, but mine also. For example, faculty members who have attended my instructional sessions have also asked me to make presentations to their classes. Students in the classes have asked me for additional training and help on researching specific computer databases that I teach to the faculty. By maintaining a commitment to this type of interaction, education and expertise in the field of library research feeds not only the patron, but also the librarian.

ment to identify themes and ideas that need clarification or revision. Also, consider forming a writing group to periodically read and review one another's drafts.

TEACHING OBJECTS AND SUPPORTING DATA

The selection and organization of documents and artifacts are based upon the purpose of the portfolio. The items selected should reflect the themes and accomplishments mentioned in the Teaching Philosophy Statement and Summary of Teaching Responsibilities. Using a table of contents is a logical approach and provides easy access for the reader to supporting documentation. A sample table of contents is featured in Exhibit E3.2.

SUPPORTING DATA

Many types of artifacts can be used as supporting data in the portfolio. Examples of supporting evidence include the following:

- Course syllabi that demonstrate library instruction needs and proficiencies
- Student work samples (research papers, worksheets, Web sites, etc.)
- Student, faculty, and peer evaluations of bibliographic instruction or reference services

- Descriptions of new and/or innovative teaching methods, instructional materials, technological innovations: handouts, technical writing samples and manuals, user guides, bibliographies, worksheets, presentation slides, etc.
- Descriptions of advising or mentoring activities
- Efforts to improve teaching such as conferences and workshops attended
- Unsolicited or solicited evaluations and commendations from students, colleagues, and researchers
- Awards or other recognition

Each item can be supplemented with an explanation of why that item was included, with a reference to the Statement of Teaching Philosophy and/or Summary of Teaching Responsibilities. Because the

---

EXHIBIT E3.2. Sample Table of Contents
Teaching Portfolio
Mark McCallon
Business Reference Librarian
Margaret and Herman Brown Library
Abilene Christian University
Fall 2005

I. Table of Contents
  A. Teaching Responsibilities
  B. Teaching Philosophy
  C. Teaching Methods, Strategies, Innovations
    1. Handouts, Assignments, Syllabi
    2. Student Work Samples
    3. Flyers and Brochures Pertaining to Workshops and Presentations
  D. Ratings and Recognition
    1. Student, Faculty and Peer Evaluations
    2. Unsolicited or Solicited Evaluations from Students and Faculty
    3. Awards and other Recognition
  E. Efforts to Improve Teaching
    1. Conferences or Workshops Attended
    2. Revisions in Handouts or Teaching Methods
    3. Teaching Goals—Short- and Long-Term
  F. Appendixes

portfolio is a living document, supporting artifacts can be added or removed depending on the purpose of the evaluation. For annual evaluations, a two-year time span of materials can be included. For tenure and promotion a longer time span of up to six or seven years can be covered.

USES OF THE PORTFOLIO

As more institutions of higher education have adopted the teaching portfolio as a mechanism to evaluate and promote teaching effectiveness, the uses have expanded to include formative and summative. The summative use of the portfolio is for personnel decisions, such as tenure or promotion. A well-designed, standardized portfolio provides evidence that an administrator or faculty member outside of the discipline can identify with. As an added by-product, a faculty member is able to learn something about other disciplines and unfamiliar teaching methods. A formative use of the portfolio is the improvement of teaching. The portfolio allows the reference librarian to reflect on practices and tools that acknowledge the role of teaching in the classroom setting and individual instruction at the reference desk. Moreover, the materials selected for inclusion in the portfolio spur the librarian on to self-improvement.

CONCLUSION

The shift of reference services from a primarily service-oriented role to a teaching role has opened new doors for librarians to collaborate with faculty and to demonstrate effective teaching practices at the reference desk and in the classroom. As librarians utilize assessment tools and pedagogical strategies to encourage learning in the academic library, it is imperative to reflect upon and document the importance of teaching. The teaching portfolio is a valuable instrument for organizing what has been learned from teaching activities and apply the evidence to improve instructional programs.

NOTE

1. Seldin, Peter. *The Teaching Portfolio,* Third Edition. Boulton, MA: Anker Publishing Company, 2004.

BIBLIOGRAPHY

Arnold, Judith M. and Pearson, Karen B. Using the Teaching Portfolio to Define and Improve the Instructional Role of the Academic Librarian. In Linda Shirato and Rhonda Fowler (Eds.), *Change in Reference and BI: How Much Help and How?* (pp. 29-42). Ann Arbor, MI: Pierian Press, 1996.

Lally, Ann. Teaching Portfolios and the Continuous Improvement of Teaching. *Art Documentation* 19(1) (2000): 48-49.

Lally, Ann and Trejo, Ninfa. Creating the Developmental Teaching Portfolio: A Great Tool for Self-Assessment. *College and Research Libraries News* 59(10) (November 1998): 776-778.

Saunders, Laura. Professional Portfolios for Librarians. *College and Undergraduate Libraries* 10(1) (2003): 53-59.

Tuttle, Jane P. Bringing the "Invisible" into Focus: Teaching Portfolios for the Instruction Librarian. In Julia K. Nims and Ann Andrew (Eds.), *Library User Education in the New Millennium: Blending Tradition, Trends, and Innovation* (pp. 141-149). Ann Arbor, MI: Pierian Press, 2001.

EXERCISES

1. Summarize this essay, stating the main points for a classmate or co-worker who knows very little about the subject or has not read the essay. Relate this essay to your experience as a student, employee, or customer.
2. Rewrite the summary for a different audience (expert in the field, college administrator, fund-raiser).
3. With a classmate or co-worker, role-play the essay, with one person playing the author, and the other person asking the author about his or her purpose, motivations, main points, evidence, conclusions, etc.
4. Do you agree or disagree with the main points of this essay? Do you base this on prior knowledge, opinion, author's arguments, cited evidence, intuition, or a combination of these elements?

5. Find two scholarly, authoritative sources (books or articles) that support or refute the main points of this essay. Detail the sources consulted and the search terms used.
6. If you have not already done so, start to collect and organize materials related to projects, papers, publications, and other intellectual products suitable for a yearly evaluation or promotion review.
7. Develop three to five interview questions that could be used to interview a practicing academic librarian who has developed an academic portfolio for promotion and tenure purposes.
8. Ask several colleagues (including one nonlibrarian) who have recently sought promotion and tenure to show you their academic portfolios. Compare the contents of each portfolio against evaluation guidelines established by the promotion and tenure committee of the affiliated institution.

APPENDIX: THINKING ABOUT TEACHING AND LEARNING

This worksheet is designed to help you think about your beliefs about teaching and learning, in preparation for creating a teaching philosophy statement. While you may agree with all the statements in a category, try to narrow down to one or two that most accurately reflect your beliefs.

The role of the teacher is to

☐ Modify behavior ☐ Disseminate information
☐ Facilitate learning ☐ Counsel learners

Knowledge is

☐ Absolute ☐ Absolute, but connected
☐ Constructed individually ☐ Personal or with a group

Learning is

☐ Change in behaviors or skills
☐ Acquisition of insight and understanding

Thinking About Teaching and Learning was developed by Beth Woodard, University of Illinois at Urbana–Champaign; bswoodar@uiuc.edu. Used by permission.

☐ Construction of knowledge and social skills
☐ Acquisition of and personalization of information

The role of the learner is to

☐ Receive and respond to environment
☐ Actively process ideas
☐ Construct perspective of world, solve problems
☐ Take responsibility for own learning

Student motivation is

☐ External
☐ Internal
☐ Both external and internal

The kind of thinking I want students to demonstrate includes the following:

☐ Concrete   ☐ Abstract
☐ Group meaning   ☐ Personal meaning

I know students have learned when

☐ I see them exhibit certain behaviors.
☐ I see them apply what they have learned in new contexts.
☐ I hear them explain it to someone else.
☐ I hear them explain how it impacts them personally.

When I am teaching

☐ I cover the required content accurately and in the allotted time.
☐ I ask a lot of questions.
☐ I involve the students in problem solving.
☐ I link the subject matter with real settings or practice of application.

My favorite teaching strategies are

☐ Lecture   ☐ Group discussion
☐ Active learning   ☐ Independent practice

Great teachers are:

☐ Knowledgeable experts   ☐ Creative
☐ Challenging   ☐ Inspirational, enthusiastic

My favorite way to test student learning is

- ☐ Examinations for knowledge acquisition
- ☐ Research papers or essays that ask students to connect ideas
- ☐ Case studies or group projects to solve problems
- ☐ Application of principles to a personal problem, or student reflection

A metaphor to describe my teaching would be "Being a teacher is like being a . . ."

- ☐ *Sheep dog* because . . .
- ☐ *Cook* because . . .
- ☐ *Coach* because . . .
- ☐ *Gardener* because . . .

Essay 4

The Glass of Fashion: Librarianship for the Twenty-First Century

Susan Swords Steffen
Michael J. Bell

Th' expectancy and rose of the fair state
The glass of fashion and the mold of all form

Ophelia to Hamlet [3.1.166-167]

INTRODUCTION

Contemporary college librarians can certainly identify with Ophelia's chastening of Hamlet for being "the glass of fashion," especially when they remember that she was reminding him and us to view assertions of radical cultural transformation with skepticism. Still, they also recognize that they and their profession face exciting and sometimes daunting challenges from the fashions of the day. On the one hand, college libraries are rapidly being transformed in reality and public perception from "book warehouses" to Internet-driven, information-rich environments that allow faculty and students to interact with the world from a desktop. On the other hand, reference librarians find themselves called upon to develop new skills both as teachers of critical learning skills and as research collaborators who are expected to implement complex information literacy learning programs and to cope with the increased demands of technologically sophisticated patrons for unlimited access to the information revolution. Not surprisingly, the result has been a torrent of words promot-

An Introduction to Reference Services in Academic Libraries
© 2006 by The Haworth Press, Inc. All rights reserved.
doi:10.1300/5634_15

ing the disappearance of the library, the redundancy of the librarian, and their simultaneous absolute necessity. Equally unsurprising, the result has been a serious rethinking of the form and function of the college library and of the roles of contemporary college librarians.

THE NEW LIBRARY: MYTH AND REALITY

Contemporary fashion's boldest myth that the library is fast disappearing has a long tradition. With each new technological innovation of the twentieth and twenty-first centuries, critics seek a replacement for the book and argue that innovation will drive out the past, but this myth of the mechanical confuses technological change with cultural change and the machine with the information it transmits. Somehow, the myth asserts, printing or photography or film or television or the Internet removes the power of rhetoric from intellectual communication. Somehow, the myth promises that technology will both simplify access and remove the need for interpretation. Somehow, it promises to allow an audience to see the words on its own, to view the pictures in private, to stare at the screen alone, and not be swayed by the "honeyed words" of a Cicero or seduced by the speed of Google. At its worst, the myth asserts the ultimate illusion of the democratic: immediate, instant access with no interference from anyone or anything at any time, anywhere.

Reality is far less apocalyptic, but libraries are at risk nonetheless. Substantial changes have occurred in libraries and in what librarians do. Library users have access to an enormously increased body of information. Faculty and students have become their own information gatherers and managers, yet most are operating in an information culture subject to hidden persuasions without realizing that they are being sold or occasionally manipulated. Millions of Web sites crammed with facts, opinions, falsehoods, and outright lies are a keystroke away unfiltered by a professor's insights, a librarian's awareness, or a publisher's review. Hundreds of popular magazines and professional journals that were only available at large research institutions are now accessible for review and research even at the smallest college library. The books of the great libraries of the world are or will soon be digitized and able to be read from a computer screen anywhere.[1]

As well, the cost of unlimited access is growing exponentially. Today, libraries are often expected to buy ownership, access, and the technology to make it all work. And, librarians are still expected to walk patrons to the book on the shelf, while they explain how to use the simplest and the most complex search engines, and repair the computers and printers throughout the library. Finally, college presidents and deans, who ought to know better, are buying into the media frenzy and seeing the possibility of cutting a unit that appears a drain on limited resources. Why pay for an outdated library, they say? Why not, they muse, just require everyone to buy their own computer and spend the money on other, "more needed" things like football fields and fitness centers.[2]

MANAGING THE WHIRLWIND

The key to surviving the whirlwind of fashion is to recognize immediately that the traditional roles and responsibilities of the librarians are not going away, though some will diminish in importance and others will rise to prominence. Books will still need to be bought. Journals will still need to be managed. Likewise the essential skills associated with moving through the library environment will still matter. Students, faculty, and administrators will still need to be taught basic research skills. However, librarians need to recognize that some of what they have considered core professional skills will have to be transformed into subjects to be taught. Librarians have always evaluated materials for worth and usability. They have always interpreted content and quality. They need now to understand that they have the added responsibility to help students to become their own evaluators of the quality of materials. After all, librarians are the primary community for whom the general process of evaluation has been a professional activity.

So, who do librarians need to be now? First and foremost, college librarians need to be the *teachers* of the learning skills critical to the information age. They cannot take comfort in demonstrating how to access information; they have to become responsible for demonstrating how to evaluate, synthesize, and communicate it. Moreover, to teach effectively, librarians will have to do more than stand in front of groups of students and explain how to use the library. They will need to learn to think less about transmitting information to compliant listeners and more about creating learning experiences which compel students to become active learners who make information literacy skills their own. Excellent information literacy teaching, like other excellent college teaching, will be more about talking and listening than showing and telling. The teaching role of librarians will also extend to their work with faculty. By collaborating with classroom faculty to match desired student learning outcomes with appropriate information literacy skills and to design assignments to facilitate the learning of those skills, librarians will teach teachers what to expect from their students. When done successfully, the teaching roles of librarians promise to transform teaching and learning by increasing the knowledge of information resources and by raising the expectations of both students and faculty. When coupled with redesigned library spaces and the marketing of library services, librarians will find themselves recognized both as teachers of information literacy skills and professors of knowledge.

Second, librarians need to transform reference service from question answering to inquiry facilitating. Just as excellent information literacy teaching focuses on talking and listening, so too will reference librarians become active guides and collaborators with students. Librarians will not be merely information wizards who know how to extract information from machines, but will be expert fellow travelers in the inquiry process who help users shape their research questions, provide an audience for talking about their ideas and information needs, and have ongoing in-depth conversations rather than brief reference interviews intended to launch students on solo voyages. As reference interactions become more collaborative than imperial, librarians will embrace professional roles similar to classroom faculty who have moved from sages on the stage to guides on the side. As with faculty, reference librarians will experience the pleasures and terrors of that paradigm shift. The easiest thing for a budding teacher to do is to construct the learning experience so that no student can fail. The teacher merely ensures success by doing all of his or her work and the students' at the same time. It is what any parent does when they start collaborating with their child and end up writing the essay or building the rocket for them. The hardest thing for a novice teacher to learn is that students must be given the opportunity to fail along with the responsibility and the tools to succeed. And no doubt, the hardest thing for the teaching librarian to accept is to watch educated students continue to flounder when it would be so simple to step in and fix the problem.

EDUCATIONAL LEADERSHIP

Finally, it is imperative that librarians seek roles as educational leaders on their campuses. Librarians' expertise in information management and the academic use of information technology is important to today's colleges and universities, and this expertise can be an effective means to bring librarians to the table. However, it will not be enough to just sit around and tell people how to use the computer or even how to tell a bad Web site from a good Web site. True educational leadership for librarians means assuming responsibility for the college's mission to educate, claiming their portion of that mission as their own, and asserting that both the mission is incomplete and the college education offered is insufficient without what librarians bring to the process. Most small, tuition-dependent colleges cannot survive only on their traditional hallmarks of small classes and intimate professor-student relationships because almost none can keep their laboratories and classrooms on the cutting edge. However, thanks to the information revolution, today's library brings the world to the classroom and the laboratory in ways unimagined a decade ago. Accordingly, librarians have the opportunity to become essential to the success of the college's mission, but only if they claim their role as educational leaders and learn to aid without being a servant.

Of course, changed responsibilities will lead inevitably to changed expectations and changed views of college librarians. But college librarians must welcome such change. The college community and the wider world do not see professors as mere support or supplement. They are seen as essential, and college librarians will need to develop new criteria to evaluate and assess the performance of librarians in this new enlightened environment. In this regard, faculty status and rank will become important for librarians not only because they provide protections in the classroom and for their scholarly and professional work, but because they allow librarians to speak as equals. With that equality comes the responsibility to assess and document the librarianship, service, and professional scholarly activities of librarians. If librarians are serious about their educational role as teachers and professors, it will be essential to assess library faculty performance in the areas of librarianship rather than to recast their librarianship in the criteria used to evaluate the performance of classroom faculty. Such an endeavor, however, will require a change in faculty and librarian consciousness and the willingness of both to acknowledge the importance of their emerging partnership.

CONCLUSION

Almost a century ago in the magazine *The Editor,* D. W. Griffith, filmmaker, imagined the end of the library this way:

> There will be long rows of boxes or pillars, properly classified and indexed, of course. At each box a push button and before each box a seat. Suppose you wish to "read up" on a certain episode in Napoleon's life. Instead of consulting all the authorities, wading laboriously through a host of books, and ending bewildered, without a clear idea of exactly what did happen and confused at every point by conflicting opinions about what did happen, you will merely seat your self at a properly adjusted window, in a scientifically prepared room, press the button, and actually see what happened. There will be no opinion expressed. You will merely be present at the making of history.[3]

Librarians may be as awed by Griffith's arrogance as they are amused by his naiveté, but they should also recognize some of our own fashionable times in his comments. The library has not gone away and it will not be going away in the near or far future. It will change as it has always done, adapting to new technologies, husbanding old skills, and teaching new ones, but what will remain most important is the recognition that the librarian at the center of it all must continue to play out his or her professional responsibility of interpreter and evaluator of what is worth preserving from all of the freight of culture. That this cannot be done by simply gathering all the books in one room is a given. That they can and must do it by teaching students, faculty, and administrators how to find, how to use, how to judge, and how to value what is good and what is the best of information and its more useful cousin, knowledge, is a necessity.

NOTES

1. Google Partners with Libraries in Massive Digitization Project. *American Libraries* 36(January) (2005): 26-27.
2. Geduld, Harry M. *Focus on D. W. Griffith*. Englewood Cliffs, NJ: Prentice-Hall, 1971, 34-35.
3. Ibid.

BIBLIOGRAPHY

Blackwell, Lewis and Carson, David. *The End of Print*. San Francisco. Chronicle Books, 2000.

Helfand, Jessica. Sticks and Stones Can Break My Bones But Print Can Never Hurt Me: A Letter to Fiona on First Reading *The End of Print*. Available at http://www.typeculture.com/academic_resource/articles_essays/pdfs/tc_article_10.pdf. Accessed August 1, 2005.

Mumford, Lewis. *Technics and Civilization*. New York: Harcourt, Brace and World, Inc., 1963.

Phipps. Shelley. Rafting the Rapids 2005: Searching for Our Purpose. *College and Research Libraries News* 66(February) (2005): 114-117.

Sapp, Gregg and Gilmour, Ron. A Brief History of the Future of Academic Libraries: Predictions and Speculations from the Literature of the Profession, 1976-2000-part two, 1990-2000. *Portal: Libraries and the Academy* 3(January) (2003): 13-25.

Wilder, Stanley. Information Literacy Makes All the Wrong Assumptions. *The Chronicle of Higher Education* (January 7, 2005): 51(18) 13.

EXERCISES

1. Summarize this essay, stating the main points for a classmate or co-worker who knows very little about the subject. Relate this essay to your experience as a student, employee, or customer.
2. Rewrite the summary for a different audience (expert in the field, college administrator, fund-raiser).
3. With a classmate or co-worker, role-play the essay, with one person playing the author, and the other person asking the author about his or her purpose, motivations, main points, evidence, conclusions, etc.
4. Do you agree or disagree with the main points of this essay? Do you base this on prior knowledge, opinion, authors' arguments, cited evidence, intuition, or a combination of these elements?

5. Find two scholarly, authoritative sources (books or articles) that support or refute the main points of this essay. Detail the sources consulted and the search terms used.
6. Based on this essay, what do you think are the most significant challenges facing academic librarians interested in becoming educational leaders or exerting educational leadership in a college or university setting?
7. Develop three to five interview questions that could be used to interview a college administrator who is convinced that libraries are obsolete.

Essay 5

Frames of Reference
Considering the Meaning
of Reference—Its Origins,
Present, and Future

Linda Loos Scarth

In this essay, I explore some of the history of the words *reference,
referee,* and *referent* and briefly refer to some of the major influences
on the practice of reference librarianship in the past 140 years while
puzzling over where we are and why the profession agonizes over its
expertise and practice. I also respectfully make some suggestions on
what academic reference librarians in particular may have to consider
as their institutions, faculties, and student bodies change.

REFERENCE/REFEREE/REFERENT

The 2004 election cycle brought the concept of language framing
to the forefront, or at least toward the front, of public discussion. We
are perhaps more aware of the nature of language in coloring ideas,
some of which may be quite the opposite of the images created by the
words used to label or describe. The word "librarian" certainly has its
own visual and psychological baggage and reference has its own history and interpretation.

Oxford English Dictionary Online (OED Online)[1] with its definitions, etymologies, and quotations provides descriptions of reference

An Introduction to Reference Services in Academic Libraries
© 2006 by The Haworth Press, Inc. All rights reserved.
doi:10.1300/5634_16

and its relatives that help to frame some of my thoughts about what it means to be a reference librarian and what it might mean in the future. It is useful to consider some of the subtleties of meaning as we reflect on the scope of reference librarianship.

The earliest entry (1589) quoted use of the word *reference* as the act of asking a person of authority to assist in settling a dispute or helping to make a decision. This is something reference librarians expect will happen when a reference interaction occurs and the librarian is the authority to whom one turns for finding information to use in making decisions. Although the act of being a reference was probably not applied to librarianship until the latter part of the nineteenth century, it is a characteristic the profession must work to retain as technology continues to alter our ways of interacting with our potential clients. I prefer client to customer/patron/user because it implies a more professional relationship. Another early variant meaning is *reference* as the standard that was used to measure. We are in the business of guiding users to information that is accurate and of a specific standard.

About the same time, other writers used reference to mean a relationship or respect between ideas, things, or persons. A bit later, reference acquired more abstract connotations in logic and linguistics where one concept carried with it meanings beyond that which was denoted. The modern reference librarian is certainly a vehicle to foster relationships between people and ideas. Although it was several hundred years before reference became an attribute of a book or a librarian, the concept of bringing together persons and information is very important. The librarian is also representative of the larger world of information and the language used to communicate it. Reference and meaning became intertwined and in doing so, one of the librarian's tasks is to help clients move through complex relationships among concepts and ideas.

Early in the seventeenth century, reference became a directional activity, presaging modern usage. It is the act of directing someone to a book, and within a book, directing readers to other sources within the document or to other documents where further information might be found. Reference lists were on the way to becoming used and disliked. By the beginning of the eighteenth century, disparaging remarks were already being made about extensive references within books.

Nineteenth-century writers added the act of referring one person to another for information or explanation, and referee came to mean more than one who settles disputes or manages activities. We can think of the modern librarian as the referee between the client and the information sources used. Sometimes this may seem like settling a dispute when information sources offer alternative views or do not agree with the client's desired answers. Along the way, meanings akin to benchmark and comparison place, object, or group were added.

My personal favorite definition is that for referent. The first definition is "one who is referred to or consulted."[2] Of course, more modern usage of referent is for the object, idea, etc., referred to in spoken or written communication. The older meaning is what every reference librarian should aspire to within the organization or community where he or she works, especially the academic reference librarian.

There are those who feel that we should stop using the word *reference* because it is not widely understood and, like much of library jargon, is understood less as time passes. Even though I proudly call myself a reference librarian, I find I am starting to add "or research librarian" to explain a bit more of what I do. A sad but telling cartoon in the December 28, 2004, issue of the *Christian Science Monitor* has a child with a laptop with a search engine home page asking the adult in the picture "What is a library?"[2]

It used to be that we could tell our clients that the library was their gateway to the Internet but that is no longer so. We now hope they find us via the Internet. Google is doing libraries a service through its indexing algorithms. Perhaps we librarians need to revise our language and how we present our resources so that keyword and natural language searches on the World Wide Web will more often find the more authoritative resources we provide.

Although those of us who see in reference librarianship many of the characteristics of reference and referee, one must note that *OED* has little to say about the reference librarian with more attention paid to books, rooms, and buildings. In fact, the first (and obsolete) definition of librarian is "scribe, copyist." The second is "the keeper or custodian of a library" which replaced "library-keeper." It has long puzzled me why our culture confuses the library as building with the librarian as person and professional. Perhaps the person of the librarian became seen as an extension of the building and collection rather than one who uses the building and collection to accomplish specific useful and valuable tasks. Early writers rarely discussed the librarian as the professional to whom one referred, but more likely mentioned the texts that resided in buildings and the obligation of library assistants or librarians to get "readers" to the right section in the library. Sometimes there was reference to the learned nature of librarians and "librarianesses." They may be learned but they must not put that knowledge to great use by doing library research.

FRAMES

Framing happens to everything from buildings and paintings to countries, decisions, issues, policy actions, news analyses, and information of any type. Linguists and social theorists use the concept to study how and why framing influences outcomes. Politicians are masterful at framing issues, sometimes to confuse doubters and sometimes to fit the needs of supporters. Librarians also create frames whether they are concerned with resisting stereotypes, ways of conducting business, coming to terms with professionalism, and their relationship with clients.

Librarians have framed descriptions of what they do (or should do) for the past 140 years and sometimes have criticized the profession for not fitting into particular frames. Extrapolating from the definitions of reference, refer, and referee found in *OED* was an exercise to frame what I think should be a reevaluation of earlier frames and to encourage new frames as we develop ever-widening expertise and responsibility. Librarian scholars writing in the late nineteenth and early twentieth century and the development of the Library of Congress in the same period did much to establish the frames in which reference librarians work and behave. These frames have both established the profession and potentially inhibit it from evolving with the changes in culture in relation to information seeking. Rather than reiterate these descriptions of reference service beyond several brief points, I recommend Rabner and Lorimer's article *Definitions of Reference Service: A Chronological Bibliography.*[3] Other writers[4-7] are recommended for review of our history and present state.

One of the striking features of descriptions of the Library of Congress's reading room 100 to 125 years ago is that it admitted only "potential readers" who made requests for specific items.[8] Reader assistance and support grew out of the questions asked during the last years of the nineteenth century. Administrators guarded against employees offering too much assistance. The policy was to just tell them what the best literature is and where it is in the library.

Considered one of the parents of modern reference service, Ainsworth Spofford cautioned in 1900 that librarians leave readers to their own search after putting the resources before them so that they would become self-sufficient researchers. This frame of mind is still prevalent and is one which I believe needs to be examined and modified if reference librarians are to fulfill their potential as professionals in a world drowning in information, misinformation, and propaganda of infinite variety. The world needs rigorous minds with a love of the chase and puzzle-solving skills while sorting information. The abilities to think critically about, verify, and cross-check information should become valuable commodities. Reference librarians frequently possess these characteristics by temperament, education, available resources, and the opportunity to stay ahead of the learning curve as the resources and technologies change.

Reference librarians need to be excellent information researchers and may need to offer more of this service to remain "referents." A librarian-researcher can search efficiently for and provide desired information to an appreciative clientele. As the information literacy fad seems to be waning in the library literature, I observe that one of the changes in reference and instructional service is that there is less rather than more interest in learning to be a highly skilled information source user, both by students and faculty.

Information gathering is outsourced to search engines and if required, to the database aggregators. Painstaking searches for information with the inevitable circuitous routes, cul-de-sacs, and interesting side roads do not fit in a linear world where the object is to get from point A to point B by the most direct route. These attitudes are reinforced by public education policy and our culture's commodity mind-set. It is not that students do not want to find and use information but that they want to find it in the most direct way with the least effort and expect all of it to be of acceptable value. Learning about the nuances of information, disinformation, propaganda, and search precision is of little interest or value. Technologies change so fast that they feel it is pointless to learn the many approaches to information research because the approaches will change before they need it again. The simple, direct, and unambiguous approach will do. The underlying concepts that would serve them well as technologies change are more abstract than many clients care to learn. These comments are more a realistic description than a lament. It is the way of the world that must be worked around.

How should reference librarians respond when asked, "What do you do?" I suggest that we respond with a firm, "Any information research that needs to be done and answering any question that comes our way" in our places of employment. This includes among other things, the preparation of bibliographies of all important papers about a topic that will be used by a faculty researcher preparing a review of literature or a new course. It also means talking a nervous computer user through the login instructions to the campus intranet. Or, it can be uploading materials to course pages on the campus course management server. None of these fit in the older frames of reference service but are ways to be the referent in the lives of our workplaces. We establish our usefulness, value, and credibility by being the ones referred to in many senses of that word. Faculty members are our best potential clients. When they use any or all of our services successfully, they are more likely to expect students to do the same.

Personally, I like to think that part of my job is being the referee between our students (also, faculty and staff) and the huge number of resources available for any particular task. Frustrated students frequently ask for me to be the referee between themselves and the computer, periodical databases, catalog, Library of Congress subject headings and call numbers, and publication types (scholarly, professional, and popular), college course management system, and much more.

More frequently than I would like, I encounter a student who says, "I found everything I need for this assignment on the Web but my instructor says we have to use three journal articles and one book. I can't find the journal articles on the library Web page. Please help." When we finish, the "Wow, that was not so bad" response is both reward and red flag. Library language does not frame information in meaningful ways for our students, leading me to change the link on our library Web page from "Periodical Indexes and Other Databases" to "Journals, Magazines, Newspapers, and Online Books." This simple change seems to get students to the indexes and databases without their knowing it.

REFRAMING REFERENCE

As a college reference librarian where the library is the center for information technology on campus, reference service refers to any question, information, or information technology need that comes in the door, over the telephone, through e-mail, or wherever we are on campus. This is not just the case for me but for each of us that works here. We all enjoy and thrive on learning new technologies, trouble-shooting minor computer issues, teaching about resources, and more often, putting the appropriate resources where students and faculty will stumble upon them if they have not been deliberate in finding and using them. The campus community expects that full service from the library includes information technology as well as information.

Many information sources are available through the library and most people will accept the first and easiest source they encounter. Making as many of the resources easily accessible is one of the library's most important reference and technological activities. This is partly because most students are really only part-time scholars even when carrying a full complement of course hours.

Years ago when I taught child development at a university, we often talked with our students about the jobs of children of various ages and stages. The job of young children is to play and the job of the six- to eighteen-year-old is to go to school. At that time, the job of the college student was to go to college and truly be a student. The jobs for all ages have changed and are continuing to do so. Taking courses is just a small part of the lives of most college students. Faculty are often sympathetic to students' lives and priorities and have adjusted instruction and expectations in response to this societal change. Faculty, too, cannot keep up with the burgeoning and ever-changing information resources available through a college library. Therefore, in my opinion, reference librarians should rethink their role as guides to learning how to find and evaluate information and think more about assisting in the educational process by making it easy to get to the most authoritative information for any and all disciplines. We need to put it where it is hard to ignore: on the campus portal home page; individual student, faculty, and staff course management system pages; faculty/staff intranet; and desktops all over campus.

In fall 2004 there was a lengthy thread on an e-mail discussion group about the technical skills needed by reference librarians. Most of the skills shared with the group were rather routine and somewhat pedestrian. They seemed more related to tools than to using knowledge of those tools to help people having trouble using them. Perhaps I missed it, but no one spoke of the skill for assisting clients in using computer and information technologies so they could use library resources more effectively. I was struck that while the skills list is quite long and so different than reference service 100 years ago or even twenty-five years ago,[9] the attitude is much the same: point people to information but do not help them very much. I do not believe that most reference librarians just point in their practice but that they are afraid to admit in front of one another that they can and do solve technological and informational problems for their clients. The shadows falling from the nineteenth century frames are dense and powerful.

Libraries and librarians have undergone several metamorphoses from ancient times to the present and I believe must continue to do so to be relevant and funded by parent organizations. For most of the history of libraries and librarianship, libraries were places for the already learned to continue their privileged intellectual position. Even after libraries evolved to become educational institutions for a wider slice of the population, readers were on missions of self-education (sometimes with the recommendations of the librarian as arbiter of what was worthwhile—remember "Marian the Librarian" in *The Music Man*). Academic libraries next became the place to gather information to complete course assignments, with and without librarian assistance. In the past several decades, college libraries were often among the first units on campus to offer Internet access. Libraries (and the business office and registrar) were the place where information technologies found practical application for more than computer "nerds" (now "geeks"). As information technologies have become ubiquitous, the need for expert information management and searching has increased while the general skill is not keeping pace. Reference librarians can provide the skill to their potential clients when we get past just showing how to deliver superior products.

These two polar impulses—providing fine resources but only directing people too them—are still alive and, while not as well as in the past, still frame many people's concept of reference service. Although I agree with Bowness[10] that librarians need to become better at the public relations and advertising aspects of their professions and that the eight behaviors she recommends are all important and achievable, I think it is key to practice a variation of behavior number two on her list—becoming the information go-to person. Reference librarians should use their resources to provide well-searched and packaged answers to many of the questions without necessarily encouraging clients to do it themselves. Library use will increase if the work can be outsourced to the professional librarian. We need to be research librarians and information specialists who infiltrate the places our clientele use rather than only tempting them to come to us. They only come to us and our workplaces when the need can only be satisfied there or they get better service and results from our expertise. I suggest that to truly put reference, refer, and referent into librarianship, even with more widely understood names, and maintain credibility and increase our professionalism, we need to assist people in using the technologies, deliver information to clients in their own environments, and provide the physical and electronic library. One definition of a professional is a member of a learned occupation who offers advice and expertise to others and keeps up to date on the methods and materials used in doing so. Librarians are praised for being early adopters of information technology. Now we must earn praise for interpreting the technologies and using those technologies to provide full-service research and reference services to our clients.

The word "reference" has a long lineage and many meanings. It is time to expand the information-researcher component of reference and define the reference librarian as the one who searches, finds, organizes, evaluates, and provides the most credible information to clients in a form and at a time and place that augments their productivity. Librarians need to do all this while occasionally teaching some of the requisite skills to those open to learn. We need to professionally do what we do best: be the information referent in our workplaces.

NOTES

1. *Oxford English Dictionary Online*. Available by subscription at http://dictionary.oed.com. Accessed August 1, 2005.

2. Stahler, Stanley. What's A Library. [political cartoon]. *Christian Science Monitor.* December 27, 2004, p. 9.

3. Rabner, Lanell and Lorimer, Suzanne, comp. *Definitions of Reference Service: A Chronological Bibliography.* Available at http://www.ala.org/ala/rusa/rusaourassoc/rusasections/mouss/moussection/mousscomm/evaluationofref/refdef bibrev.pdf. Accessed August 1, 2005.

4. Genz, Marcella D. Working the Reference Desk. *Library Trends,* 46(3) (1998): 505-525.

5. Gorman, Michael. Values for Human-to-Human Reference. *Library Trends* (Fall 2001). Available at http://www.findarticles.com/p/articles/mi_m1387/is_2_50/ai_83342852/print. Accessed August 1, 2005.

6. Janes, Joseph. *Introduction to Reference Work in the Digital Age.* New York: Neal-Schuman Publishers, 2003.

7. Tyckoson, David. *On the Desirableness of Personal Relations Between Librarians and Readers: The Past and Future of Reference Service.* The Future of Reference Services Papers. Available at http://www.ala.org/ala/rusa/rusaprotools/futureofref/desirableness.htm. Accessed August 1, 2005.

8. Nelson, Josephus. *Full Circle: Ninety Years of Service in the Main Reading Room.* Washington, DC: Center for the Book, Library of Congress, 1991.

9. Rabner and Lorimer, *Definitions of Reference Service.*

10. Bowness, Sue. Librarians vs. Technology. *Information Highways* (November-December 2004). Available at http://www.econtentinstitute.org/. Accessed August 1, 2005.

EXERCISES

1. Summarize this essay, stating the main points for a classmate or co-worker who knows very little about the subject, or who has not read the essay. Relate this essay to your experience as a student, employee, or customer.

2. Rewrite the summary for a different audience (expert in the field, college administrator, fund-raiser).

3. With a classmate or co-worker, role-play the case study, with one person playing the author, and the other person asking the author about his or her purpose, motivations, main points, evidence, conclusions, etc.

4. Do you agree or disagree with the main points of this essay? Do you base this on prior knowledge, opinion, author's arguments, cited evidence, intuition, or a combination of these elements?

5. Find two scholarly, authoritative sources (books or articles) that support or refute the main points of this essay. Detail the sources consulted and the search terms used.

6. Based on this essay, what do you think are the most significant challenges facing academic librarians interested in planning, managing, or evaluating reference services?

7. Develop three to five interview questions that could be used to interview a practicing academic librarian about his or her experience as a referee, referent, and reference librarian.

Essay 6

Serving Unusual Patrons
in the Library

James Langan

New librarians and library school students, yet to experience the eccentric or unusual patron in a public service work environment, may benefit from discussion within the professional literature and in library school about how best to assist this user. This topic seems to be rarely discussed, until a librarian has that rare experience.

Over the past ten years, I have occasionally assisted some rather unusual library patrons. Perhaps this should be expected when you work at the reference desk. Most classes in library school treat the subject of unusual patrons in only a cursory fashion. I hope that this essay will encourage new librarians to think about how you will react to the eccentric or unusual patron. Most library users I have assisted in public services over the years have not been particularly memorable, but simply individuals looking for a tidbit of information. Only a few stand out as users with a quality you might describe as unusual. This essay is not intended to dissuade you from working in public services, but only to prepare you better by relating some of these experiences. Names have been changed and any resemblance to users in your library is only accidental.

Sometimes a library user will surprise you. I never really noticed "Tin Foil Hat" until the day I first assisted him. For more than a year he had been just one of the library's Sunday-afternoon regulars. Wearing a sport coat and tie, and carrying a briefcase, he could have been a professor at any university. One afternoon the library's student assistant informed us that one of the patrons was wearing a tin foil hat. Thinking it had to be a prank, one of the librarians went back into

An Introduction to Reference Services in Academic Libraries
© 2006 by The Haworth Press, Inc. All rights reserved.
doi:10.1300/5634_17

the periodical stacks. Yep, she was right. Seated at one of the study carrels was a man with *The New York Times*. He was reading quietly, so the librarian walked past him.

Fashioned from aluminum foil, the rumpled cone-shaped hat must have been about a foot tall. It appeared the aluminum was wrapped around something either to protect his head or to stiffen the foil. About thirty minutes later he walked past the information desk without the hat. We presumed he had folded the hat and placed it in his briefcase.

Although he continued to use the library regularly, we never saw him with this hat on again. Naturally, one must wonder why he wore the hat that afternoon. As a new librarian, I had become used to students doing unusual things (such as spiked and dyed hair, and body piercing), but didn't usually see adults doing this type of thing. If you see a library patron suddenly do something unusual, do your best to focus on the user's question and the assistance you are there to provide. Remember, we cannot deny services to patrons because of their appearance. It is important for librarians and staff to be familiar with their library's policy about difficult patrons, but this normally applies to the boisterous or unruly individual.

Sometimes, it's not the patron's appearance that is unusual, but his or her actions. Another experience I became aware of was a patron who exhibited some traits that might be described as a little paranoid. This individual was convinced that one of his relatives had run afoul of a local organized crime syndicate. He spent the better part of a year trying to find articles about this relative in the microfilmed archive of the local newspaper and print copies of *LIFE* magazine. When he was unable to find an article on the subject, he insisted the crime syndicate must have selectively edited the articles from both *LIFE* and the local newspaper. There were gaps in the library's newspaper holdings, due to the 1936 St. Patrick's Day flood, which resulted in over seventy buildings in the city being destroyed, and thousands more damaged. The gap, however, was more likely caused by an act of God rather than organized crime.

Students may have possibly caused the gaps he found in *LIFE* magazine. Some photos and a few articles had been surreptitiously removed from the magazine. It is not likely that organized crime was involved in this. It was probably frugal students who did not want to pay for photocopying the article or photo they wanted. Library staff offered to assist the user find the information in another resource by looking up the missing story in *Readers' Guide to Periodical Literature,* but he did not want to provide us with more detail, such as the names of those involved.

While perusing the newspapers on microfilm, he continued to look around regularly, apparently to guard against those who might be near him. If anyone came close to the screen he would try to block the screen with his body. He had previously telephoned the library a few times attempting to find information. But, because he was afraid his phone was tapped, he indicated he could not give the reference librarian much information. Those reference interviews were not as productive as they could have been. Sometimes a library patron wants to find answers very badly, but may not be comfortable sharing information with anyone offering assistance. Let the patron tell you as much as he or she is comfortable with, however, if he or she does not want to share more you must respect his or her privacy.

Sometimes library patrons do not really want to find information. They just want someone to listen to them. They may be lonely and want to talk to someone. If you are working in a public area you have a responsibility to listen to them.

A patron fitting this description reappeared in the library after a three-month absence. He is not violent or boisterous, but he can be a little disconcerting. As he walked through the library it was noticed he had changed his hair. His usual tangled mass of hair was not falling off the back of his head to his shoulders, but instead was twirled up on top of his head in a spiked fashion.

One of the librarians was reshelving books in the reference section. "Excuse me," the patron said, "You know that President Bush and Kerry are on the same team don't you?" He then launched into a rambling discourse on politics and society. It was something about Bush and Kerry both working with Russian President Putin. The real power in the world, he stated, was China and, "they are going to take over!" According to him, the USSR did not dissolve in 1992. "The fall of communism is a lie told to us by . . . ." At times, it sounded like he had swallowed a dictionary and was stringing words together. "God does exist but even if he did not exist he would exist. I know because last week I was having an out of body experience . . . ." he continued. After about five minutes, he nodded to the librarian, said thank you, and returned to the stacks.

Regardless of appearance, if a library patron wants to speak with us it is important—we have a responsibility to listen respectfully and offer the best service possible. As long as the patron is not interfering with critical responsibilities, we should be as patient as possible. Even if you don't agree with the political or social views they may expound upon, listen politely. Although they may be looking for information, the patron may also just want someone to acknowledge their needs.

Sometimes there are limits to what you can do to help a patron. Sandy was a regular user of the library. Usually she would come to the library to access the *U.S. Code*. Occasionally, she would speak to the librarian about legal questions. Often we would listen politely, but then have to tell her that we couldn't answer her question. We could only suggest that she contact a lawyer. Taking our advice, she would compile a list of local lawyers and call the library to ask for their phone numbers. Later she gave up on local lawyers, as she had acquired a list of lawyers in a nearby state and wanted phone numbers for several of them. After the librarian found a Web directory that listed her chosen lawyer's names and phone numbers, she announced that she also wanted the address and phone number for the U. S. attorney general. Although we have wondered what she was involved in that required the attorney general's help, it was not appropriate to ask.

No matter how unusual a patron's query may seem, it is important that we be respectful and not make the question seem unimportant. We must always try our best to find the information.

Sooner or later, the new librarian will meet an unusual patron. No matter what they may look like or how odd their question may seem, we must offer respect to all patrons. Although your initial urge may be to avoid the eccentric or unusual patron, you should suppress it and look past the eccentricities to the patron's need. Understand that they are people who are looking for information, validation, or just someone to listen. By speaking with some of the senior librarians, you may learn about some of your library's more unusual patrons. You might ask senior librarians if they can offer helpful tips on assisting the unusual patron.

EXERCISES

1. Summarize this essay, stating the main points for a classmate or co-worker who knows very little about the subject, or who has not read the essay. Relate this essay to your experience as a student, employee, or customer.
2. Rewrite the summary for a different audience (expert in the field, college administrator, fund-raiser).
3. With a classmate or co-worker, role-play the essay, with one person playing the author, and the other person asking the author about his or her purpose, motivations, main points, evidence, conclusions, etc.
4. Do you agree or disagree with the main points of this essay? Do you base this on prior knowledge, opinion, author's arguments, cited evidence, intuition, or a combination of these elements?
5. Find two scholarly, authoritative sources (books or articles) that support or refute the main points of this essay. Detail the sources consulted and the search terms used.
6. Based on this essay, what do you think are the most significant challenges facing academic librarians who encounter disruptive or unusual patrons?
7. Develop three to five interview questions that could be used to interview a practicing academic librarian about his or her experience handling disruptive or unusual patrons.

Essay 7

The Academic Librarian

Paula M. Smith

Academic librarians are entities unto themselves, dedicated to increasing the knowledge of their campus community and expanding the library and information science literature through published articles. Academic librarians teach, provide reference assistance, publish, give presentations to industry and public audiences, and serve (in the form of committee work) the university and the community at large.

The state of academic librarianship (and most library positions) has changed with the recent arrival of technology to librarianship. From accessing electronic resources with inconsistent user interfaces to the advent of a "Google nation," technology has added diversity to the position of the academic librarian. It has given new meaning to efficiently accessing information and made it available to global audiences.

As a fairly new academic librarian, I stumbled out of graduate school into my position feeling totally unprepared and concerned that in time I would be "found out" and returned to the curb. I was daunted by having to teach and consort with "academics" that would judge whether I would remain at my institution, all while having to develop a research agenda that would result in publications and presentations. This lay heavy on my mind every day for the first year of my job.

In time, I relaxed my self-consciousness and allowed myself the luxury of enjoying the experience. I specifically focused on learning and understanding my role in librarianship and within the academic environment. With the help of co-workers, conferences, and the will-

An Introduction to Reference Services in Academic Libraries
© 2006 by The Haworth Press, Inc. All rights reserved.
doi:10.1300/5634_18

ingness to fail I have strategically positioned myself to succeed. For those of you looking to follow the path to academe, I offer a few learned lessons.

RESEARCH SKILLS IN FIFTY MINUTES OR FEWER: TEACHING

Most colleges and universities require a library orientation for first-year students. It is marketed as an introduction to the library, bibliographic instruction, or information literacy. Its purpose is to provide a foundation for learning how to access the library's resources and consists of an overview of library policies, a demonstration of the OPAC, one or more databases, electronic reserves, and methods for evaluating Web sites, all in fifty minutes or fewer. As a neophyte to the classroom, teaching was a painful experience as I watched the students' eyes glaze over or their heads lying on the desks. Teaching was not a skill taught in library school so I mostly sped through my presentation, clicking my mouse all over the screen, and hoped the few interested students could keep up or at a minimum would refer to their handouts afterward. After much abject blundering and observing other faculty in the classroom I learned two things: I am not the only one being ignored, and many students want library and research help when they need it, not necessarily when I am scheduled to deliver it.

With this knowledge in mind, I calmed myself down and began to ask students about their assignments prior to beginning the class. This helped me deliver a lesson relevant to their needs instead of a broad stroke of basic information. I also learned to communicate to the faculty what would and would not be covered in a class due to the limited time available, and encouraged bringing classes back for additional information or having them contact me directly.

I wish I could say my classes are now engaging environments of intellectual curiosity, but since few undergraduate courses reach that pinnacle, I strive instead to reach a few, knowing that sooner or later I will meet them at the reference desk.

WRITER'S ANGST: PUBLISHING

I, like many library students, fully expected to never have to write another paper after finishing graduate school. However, by accepting an academic librarian position, this wish did not come true. Mandated to publish or perish (academe's term for "fired!") tenure-tracked academic librarians must publish, preferably in peer-reviewed journals, to retain their position at the university. Since I am rather introverted, I have a strong preference for hiding words inside my journals and not broadcasting my thoughts for scrutiny by others. The process of writing is mind-numbingly slow for me. I am severely challenged when deciding what to write. That's followed by self-defeating thoughts of whether it is of interest to anyone, and I am almost paralyzed with fear that, once submitted for publication, it will be summarily rejected. Even with this anxiety, I experience moments of joy reading a finished piece and satisfaction at knowing the work is done.

In my humble opinion, it helps to write about something you love or have a real interest in. Don't dwell on it too much, just write. Start early. Write often. The more you write the easier it gets.

LEARNING TO PLAY NICE: COMMITTEE WORK

Committees are the general structure by which the academic environment and libraries are governed. University administration and faculty are drafted to serve on committees in order to make recommendations about campus community issues and concerns. For many academic librarians participation is expected not only on library committees but also on those created by the faculty and administration. The time spent providing university governance oversight can be interesting work; however, the difficulty is knowing when and how to ecline an invitation to participate. It is not unusual to find yourself besieged by tasks associated with various committee memberships, especially if you demonstrate a willingness and aptitude for problem solving and decision making. In my short tenure as a librarian I have learned to choose my committee assignments more wisely. Early on, I scope out whether it is a working committee (lots of tasks) or one that requires occasional participation, and attempt to select those that will allow me a balance in my library responsibilities. Sometimes, saying no is not an option. More important, I remain cognizant that my tenured colleagues, on a potential committee, may also eventually reside on the committee that decides my tenure and promotion status.

THE MYSTIQUE OF THE DOSSIER

A dossier is a collection of papers giving detailed information about a particular person or subject. This concept is one of those things never mentioned in library school. For me the term always had connotations of spy and James Bond movies. The dossier essentially is a collection of every meaningful thing that you have done while employed as a faculty member at a college or university. It consists of classes you have taught, faculty and student assessments, subject guides you have created, Web sites developed, papers published, service provided, and anything you can think of that will make you look good in the eyes of the tenure and promotion committee. It details a story of your tenure at a particular institution while conveying your consistency, participation, and expertise. Given that I learned about the dossier and the tenure and promotion process in my interview, I was sufficiently daunted. A mere reading of the requirements was enough to make my head hurt. Relief came in the form of promotion and tenure workshops offered by my employer and being assigned a mentor. The workshops provided structure to what seemed to be vague requirements. My mentor helps me to navigate the tenure waters through advisement and feedback. Most helpful to me was the willingness of my colleagues to provide copies of their dossiers; having access to a finished product at different stages of the tenure process is invaluable.

HOW COME NOBODY TOLD ME THAT?
FINDING A MENTOR

When I began working in the library I felt ill equipped to perform the job. The classes I had taken had not prepared me for being a librarian; instead, I only felt ready to find and organize information. Although this is essential to the position, there is much more to becoming a librarian. To my misfortune I found myself frequently stating, "How come nobody told me that?" As fate would have it, I was assigned a mentor.

When done right, mentoring is a joint commitment. It requires willingness on the part of the mentee to receive, give consideration to, and act on the advice and guidance offered by the mentor. The mentor commits to taking the mentee under his or her wing and sharing the knowledge and expertise that he or she has developed during the course of his or her career.

Mentors are a godsend for navigating librarianship and providing advice. They are available to steer you through the sometimes difficult and confusing aspects of the profession that present obstacles to your success. Mentors assist you in becoming acclimated to the environment, provide opportunities and advice on professional development, and generally help you through the promotion and tenure process.

Although finding and choosing a mentor is a personal task, sometimes a mentor is assigned to you during the early months of your employment. A strong benefit of this association is the mentor's ability to introduce you into the network of librarians at your facility, as well as being able to meet with you on a consistent basis. Just as important as a formally assigned mentor is a mentor outside your workplace. This can take the form of a past instructor, colleague in the industry, or employer from an internship. Occasionally, there may be concerns that you are uncomfortable speaking to your internal mentor about. A second opinion never hurts.

INFORMATION GLUT: STAYING INFORMED

As a librarian, particularly a generalist, staying abreast of the trends and hot topics of the industry is a full time job. With the increase in electronic resources, blogs, Web sites, news feeds, and e-mail it is not unusual to feel inundated by the sheer volume of information coming at you. Become skilled at knowing what is important to your position in librarianship. I find reading general information sources such as *Library Journal, College & Research Libraries News,* or the ALA Web site as good approaches to understanding what is central to the industry at large. For specific areas of information I live by LISTSERVs, preferably in digest version so that it decreases the number of e-mail messages I receive. A benefit of being a librarian is the ability to efficiently access information; however, the downside is wading through everything that we identify as important and necessary to our daily personal and working lives. My approach to managing the information glut in my work life is to create folders for the data that I deem important, and review them from time to time, deleting or tossing what is not relevant to my interests. I look for ways to conserve the amount of data I receive, and focus on those areas important to my research topics, and information important to the faculty I serve.

REMEMBERING WHY I CHOSE THIS PROFESSION— IT WASN'T THE MONEY!

I arrived in librarianship as a corporate transplant by way of the dot-com era, truly jaded, disappointed, and in need of a change. Already nurturing a long-time love affair with books and all things printed, a career in librarianship seemed a perfect fit, except the salary made me want to weep. After recovering from the shock of the pay cut, becoming a librarian has been a decision for which I have had no regrets. As a librarian, I have the ability to indulge in whatever interests me at a given moment. I am surrounded by knowledge and am stimulated everyday to learn something new, whether in the form of a reference question or my own intellectual curiosity. I take pleasure in my interactions with our library patrons even when they declare, "I am a senior and I have never been in the library." Opportunities abound in being able to learn, teach, troubleshoot, negotiate, collaborate, and revel in technological inquisitiveness. When I consider the global implications of information access and the possibilities for professional development with an international component, I am beside myself. But more than all of these things, I am grateful to participate in a field that supports intellectual freedom and seeks to provide access for all.

EXERCISES

1. Summarize this essay, stating the main points for a classmate or co-worker who has not read it. Relate this essay to your experience as a student, employee, or customer.
2. Rewrite the summary for a different audience (expert in the field, college administrator, fund-raiser).
3. With a classmate or co-worker, role-play the essay, with one person playing the author, and the other person asking the author about his or her purpose, motivations, main points, evidence, conclusions, etc.
4. Do you agree or disagree with the main points of this essay? Do you base this on prior knowledge, opinion, author's arguments, cited evidence, intuition, or a combination of these elements?
5. Find two scholarly, authoritative sources (books or articles) that support or refute the main points of this essay. Detail the sources consulted and the search terms used.
6. Based on this essay, what do you think are the most significant challenges facing entry-level academic librarians?
7. Develop three to five interview questions that could be used to interview a practicing academic librarian about his or her experience adjusting to academic life.

Index

Page numbers followed by the letter "f" indicate figures; those followed by the letter "i" indicate illustrations; and those followed by the letter "t" indicate tables.

An Introduction to Reference Services in Academic Libraries
© 2006 by The Haworth Press, Inc. All rights reserved.
doi:10.1300/5634_19

Order a copy of this book with this form or online at:
http://www.haworthpress.com/store/product.asp?sku=5634

An Introduction to Reference Services in Academic Libraries

_____ in hardbound at $49.95 (ISBN-13: 978-0-7890-2957-7; ISBN-10: 0-7890-2957-X)

_____ in softbound at $29.95 (ISBN-13: 978-0-7890-2958-4; ISBN-10: 0-7890-2958-8)

190 pages plus index • Includes illustrations

Or order online and use special offer code HEC25 in the shopping cart.

COST OF BOOKS_____

POSTAGE & HANDLING_____
(US: $4.00 for first book & $1.50
for each additional book)
(Outside US: $5.00 for first book
& $2.00 for each additional book)

SUBTOTAL_____

IN CANADA: ADD 7% GST_____

STATE TAX_____
(NJ, NY, OH, MN, CA, IL, IN, PA, & SD
residents, *add appropriate local sales tax)*

FINAL TOTAL_____
(If paying in Canadian funds,
convert using the current
exchange rate, UNESCO
coupons welcome)

☐ **BILL ME LATER:** (Bill-me option is good on
US/Canada/Mexico orders only; not good to
jobbers, wholesalers, or subscription agencies.)

☐ Check here if billing address is different from
shipping address and attach purchase order and
billing address information.

Signature_____

☐ **PAYMENT ENCLOSED: $_____**

☐ **PLEASE CHARGE TO MY CREDIT CARD.**

☐ Visa ☐ MasterCard ☐ AmEx ☐ Discover
☐ Diner's Club ☐ Eurocard ☐ JCB

Account # _____

Exp. Date_____

Signature_____

Prices in US dollars and subject to change without notice.

NAME_____

INSTITUTION_____

ADDRESS_____

CITY_____

STATE/ZIP_____

COUNTRY_____ COUNTY (NY residents only)_____

TEL_____ FAX_____

E-MAIL_____

May we use your e-mail address for confirmations and other types of information? ☐ Yes ☐ No
We appreciate receiving your e-mail address and fax number. Haworth would like to e-mail or fax special
discount offers to you, as a preferred customer. **We will never share, rent, or exchange your e-mail address
or fax number.** We regard such actions as an invasion of your privacy.

Order From Your Local Bookstore or Directly From
The Haworth Press, Inc.
10 Alice Street, Binghamton, New York 13904-1580 • USA
TELEPHONE: 1-800-HAWORTH (1-800-429-6784) / Outside US/Canada: (607) 722-5857
FAX: 1-800-895-0582 / Outside US/Canada: (607) 771-0012
E-mail to: orders@haworthpress.com

For orders outside US and Canada, you may wish to order through your local
sales representative, distributor, or bookseller.
For information, see http://haworthpress.com/distributors

(Discounts are available for individual orders in US and Canada only, not booksellers/distributors.)

PLEASE PHOTOCOPY THIS FORM FOR YOUR PERSONAL USE.
http://www.HaworthPress.com   BOF06